10 Secrets

to achieving

Add/Subtract
FACT
Mastery

AND MORE

(A Commutative / Inverse Approach)

Marion W. Stuart

Illustrations
R. Matthew Stuart

© LEARNING WRAP-UPS INC.

Ideas and Methods to Help Your Students Become Achievers

A POCKET FULL OF MAGIC COINS

Amy's teacher, Mrs. Stuart, put her hand in her teaching apron pocket and informed the students she had a MAGIC COIN. She asked if anyone would like to have it. Of course Amy's hand went up along with all the other students. Then the teacher told them that the MAGIC COIN would be worth whatever they earned by working hard and learning everything they could learn. She said that some of them might only earn a 5 MAGIC COIN, but the really hard workers could earn a 100 or maybe a 200 MAGIC COIN. When asked who would like the 200 coin, all their hands went up again.

"Let me tell you something else about my MAGIC COIN," mused the teacher. "Suppose you earn the 200 coin, and tonight you decide to buy a new bike. You go to the bike store, choose the neatest, coolest bike and pay with your MAGIC COIN. You go home, ride your bike up and down the street, and when it gets dark, you put it in a safe place so it will be ready to ride tomorrow. When you get ready for bed, you put your hand in your pocket and your MAGIC COIN is back in your pocket. You know you paid for your bike. How did that MAGIC COIN get back? Each day forever after, that coin would come back to your pocket every time you spent it."

"Now, who would like my MAGIC COIN?" Of course, everyone wanted it!

Mrs. Stuart explained that the MAGIC COIN really wasn't in her pocket, but in her head and the children finally figured out that the MAGIC COIN was knowledge. They figured out that if they had knowledge, they could use it to get more knowledge, they could use it to earn money, and the next day they could use it to earn more money, and the next year, they could still use it to make their lives better. They could use their "KNOWLEDGE MAGIC COINS" for the rest of their lives. The more they learned, the more "KNOWLEDGE MAGIC COINS" they had to spend.

Amy smiled, she was pretty sure she knew what Mrs. Stuart was talking about. "My dad earned lots of KNOWLEDGE MAGIC COINS when he went to college. Last year he spent his KNOWLEDGE MAGIC COINS to build a brand new high school. That's how he earned money for our family. Now he is in charge of building a great big civic center. I think I understand. The more we know, the more money we can earn every year, or the more we can do to help other people." She thought a second... "I'm going to try to earn a **gazillion** KNOWLEDGE MAGIC COINS!"

And so she is!

This book is dedicated to CHILDREN everywhere.
May they earn "gazillions" of KNOWLEDGE MAGIC COINS and
may they have teachers who will do everything in their power to help it happen.

In recognition of my three kindergarten granddaughters, Beth, Keni and Jenna who wanted to do "Math Problems." They were the first children to prove this method works.

Thanks to the many teachers and students who have contributed ideas and suggestions and used all or part of these materials and proved them successful.

Sincere appreciation to the great staff at Learning Wrap-ups and to my precious family who have each helped in their own way.

ISBN #0-943343-70-4   10 Secrets to Achieving Add/Subtract Fact Mastery and More

TABLE OF CONTENTS

SECTION I GETTING ACQUAINTED WITH THE PROGRAM

SECTION II MATERIALS TO PHOTOCOPY

SECTION III LESSON PLANS AND SUPPORT MATERIAL

"10 SECRETS to ADD/SUBTRACT FACT MASTERY"

ABOUT THIS BOOK

Every lesson plan in this book uses the 10 SECRETS (in differing order as needed) for each set of addition/subtraction facts, along with support material to aid in the rapid memorization and usefulness of knowing the basic facts.

"10 SECRETS" has been designed to help students:

- understand the commutative property of addition and its relationship with the inverse operation of subtraction,
- memorize the addition and subtraction facts,
- understand the power of place value,
- prepare for mental math.

It is designed to build SELF-CONFIDENCE as skills are acquired; and uses coloring, along with success-oriented activities to develop the addition and subtraction facts skills needed in life. Because students will be starting this program with a wide range of abilities, it is important for teachers to choose materials appropriate for their individual students' needs.

The POWER OF THIS PROGRAM comes from

- **SHOWING STUDENTS WHAT THEY KNOW,**
- **HELPING THEM MEMORIZE QUICKLY WITH LEARNING WRAP-UPS,**
- **BUILDING SELF-CONFIDENCE IN THE BEGINNING BY GIVING THEM THE "TOUGH LOOKING EASY STUFF."**

Most of the concepts covered in this program are taught with the lesson plans for ADD/SUBTRACT 1, 2, or 3. The purpose is to focus all the mental energy on the <u>concept</u> while working with very easy add and subtract facts. Later, students will be working on the same concepts with more difficult numbers. <u>Then</u> they can concentrate on <u>numbers</u> because they already understand the concept.

Many references on speed math, mental math or estimation suggest working problems from left to right. It is recommended in this book most of the time. As students start regrouping larger numbers, specific recommendations will be made. If students have mastered the basic facts, much of what they will need to learn will fall into place quickly.

Remember, however, that you are the teacher. Judgments will have to be made for each particular child, but always work towards the greatest performance possible from every student. You may be able to speed up the program for your class or, in some cases, find it necessary to go slower. Of course, the older the students, the more you should expect.

How many days you spend and the number of worksheets that will be needed depends on where your students are mathematically when you begin the program.

Some of the pages may pose more problems than some students will be able to complete in a given time. Kids love to believe their teacher did them a favor by assigning only certain problems. Also, it is important that students learn not to be "turned off" when they see a page with "too many" problems on it. Fold the page and assign only a portion of it to do now. Students should be able to view a full page of problems as several small sections to be completed one at a time. (This is an important lesson for life.)

Ask parents and merchants for help. Sample letters are on the next page if you choose to use them. They can add extra spark to your program.

Dear Parent,   Date

In two weeks, our class will start an intensive program to master the add/subtract facts.   We need your help and support during these next ___weeks. **It is essential that your student be in attendance every day.** We will be working with fun and effective teaching tools called LEARNING WRAP-UPS, which your student will be bringing home.   Have your child show you how they are used, then do them together.   Encourage your child to do the very best possible.

Please record the amount of time spent practicing and working on the add or subtract facts at home each evening and return the slip along with the WRAP-UPS the following morning.

Students will be recognized for the amount of time they have practiced, how well they can do the LEARNING WRAP-UPS and how high they score on a written test. There is a direct correlation between time spent practicing at home and success on the tests. They do best when you get involved.

If possible, could you spend some time in the classroom with us? We need volunteers who will encourage, cheer and applaud the students every step of the way.

Thanks for your cooperation during this most important 10 DAYS.

Sincerely,   Program Starting Date
_____

- -

Please check if you can help us. Cut along dotted line and return this slip to school.

[ ] Yes, I can help! [ ] Maybe I can help. Call me at   Parent's Signature
_____   _____

- -

Dear Merchant,
In two weeks our class will start an intensive program to master the Addition/Subtraction facts. We know this program can put us a "jump ahead" in our math program. It has been very successful in other schools and we expect our students to accomplish the same goals.

We will be giving prizes for: 1. Being in attendance every day
                                 2. Reaching the mastery goals
                                 3. Practicing at home the most total time
                                 4. Making the most progress

Your support of these students with some small prizes, gift certificates, or coupons will be most appreciated. In turn, we will ask the parents to support you.

One of our volunteers or I will stop by in a few days. Thank you so much.

Teacher _____   Grade _____

School _____   Phone number_____

SECRET 1
USE LEARNING WRAP-UPS TO MEMORIZE FACTS QUICKLY

Intensive practice takes place with the use of Learning Wrap-ups. Wrap-ups are a set of 10 5" tall plastic boards, an inch and a half wide, which have the problems on the left side and answers on the right. A string is drawn from the problems to the correct answers, and if the string covers the lines on the back of the board, the answers are all correct. (INSTANT CORRECTION and FEEDBACK.) The Learning Wrap-up technique for learning is called "SEE, SAY, WRAP-UP, WRITE." If you do not have Learning Wrap-ups, check with your local education supply store or call 1-800-992-4966 to find out how you may purchase them.

LEARNING WRAP-UPS are essential to the success of this program.

HOW TO USE WRAP-UPS

1. Loosen string at bottom of the #1 Addition WRAP-UP and unwrap.

2. Hold Wrap-ups by placing thumb at the **top**.

Younger children resist holding the Wrap-up at the top. Be patient, but keep encouraging them to hold it correctly. It will allow them to work and think faster later on.

3. Draw string **around back** of Wrap-up and up to the top number on the left which is 3. Read "3 + 1" (the add sign and the number 1 in the center of the board), then find the sum, which is 4, on the right hand side.

4. Draw string to it, then around back of board and up to the next number on the left, which is 6.

5. Continue from top down to the bottom, one number at a time and secure string in notch at the bottom. **If string covers each line on the back of the board**, ANSWERS ARE CORRECT. (Saves correction time!)

Get out your timer or watch the clock. How fast can a Wrap-up be wrapped? Older students should have a goal time of 30 seconds or less. Younger ones need more time. First and second graders should not be timed until they have developed the coordination and confidence to do it in a minute or less.

HOW TO GET WRAP-UPS READY TO USE

1. Have **students** carefully undo string bundle and unwind. (If you are teaching 1st or 2nd graders, ask for help from the upper grades.)

2. Hold end of the bundle of string in one hand and pull ONE STRING AT A TIME from the opposite end.

3. Thread about one inch of string through the hole in the Wrap-up and **tie a double or square knot**. DO NOT CUT OFF EXCESS STRING. It is already the correct length.

4. Wrap string around the board and pull end through the slit at the bottom of the board.

   - Collect the extra strings.
   - You do not need to wrap to the correct answers at this time.

TO PUT AWAY
STUDENTS wrap string around Wrap-ups, draw the last inch up through slit at the bottom. Put Wrap-ups in order, 1-10. **TEACHER places sets in storage container.**

SECRET 2
CREATING "LEARNING MAGIC" WITH DOLLARS, DIMES AND PENNIES

All students understand a little bit about money. The older your students, the easier it is to teach with this concept. Real pennies work well because they are easy to slide around, pick up and keep track of. They are almost as inexpensive as other manipulatives. You can get by with only 20 pennies per student. Have students work with the DDP (Dollars, Dimes and Penny) chart, p. 21 and also use the 100 circles chart, p. 20 to help them understand the value of one hundred (a dollar). There is a page of substitute money, p. 22, with directions that can be used if necessary.

In the beginning, the younger students should use pennies with every problem they do. The teacher can extend activities with this and the 100 Circles chart as long as is necessary.

Teach students that what they know about adding pennies (numbers in the 1's column) can be used in the dimes and dollars (10's and 100's) columns as well. Place value is the natural extension of "Dollar, Dime and Penny" activities.

SAMPLES

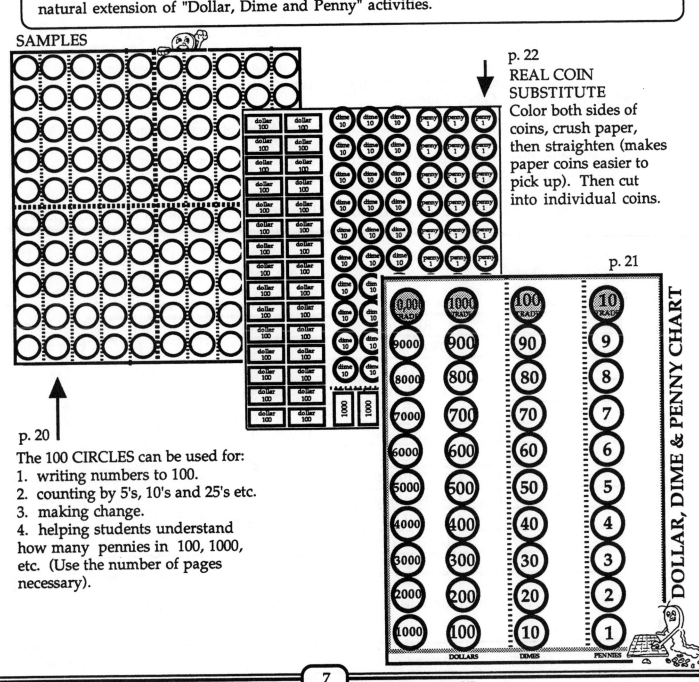

p. 22
REAL COIN SUBSTITUTE
Color both sides of coins, crush paper, then straighten (makes paper coins easier to pick up). Then cut into individual coins.

p. 21

DOLLAR, DIME & PENNY CHART

p. 20

The 100 CIRCLES can be used for:
1. writing numbers to 100.
2. counting by 5's, 10's and 25's etc.
3. making change.
4. helping students understand how many pennies in 100, 1000, etc. (Use the number of pages necessary).

SECRET 3

SHOW WHAT THEY KNOW IN COLOR (MATHNIQUE COLORING)
Coloring the MATH FACTS CHART helps students visualize the value of under-standing commutative property and the inverse operation. It shows them how quickly they can learn when they approach the addition and subtraction facts with this system.

SEEING WHAT WE KNOW IN COLOR

• Help students to see how quickly they can learn when they approach the addition and subtraction facts with this system. It shows how fast they can learn when they understand commutative properties and the inverse operation.

• Before starting the program, you may choose to give each student a copy of HERE'S WHAT I'VE LEARNED, p.18, and the MATHNIQUE COLOR CHART below. (Mathnique Coloring is a trademarked method of using color to show students what they know.)   The add/subtract chart on the cover of this book is colored with MATHNIQUE COLORING system.

• Point out that as the problems get harder, there are fewer of them to learn.

• Tell students they will be using the Mathnique Coloring system to help them understand how much they have learned about the add and subtract facts.

• **Show students there are 288 addition/subtraction problems on the chart, p.18 .**

1. Color all of the addition problems with the indicated addend, and the inverse operation.	2. Color them.	3. Number of problems and answers colored.	4. Number of problems remaining uncolored.
Addends 1	RED	46	242
10	ORANGE	42	200
11	GOLD	38	162
2	YELLOW	34	128
12	LIME GREEN	30	98
3	GREEN	26	72
4	BLUE GREEN	22	50
5	LIGHT BLUE	18	32
6	DARK BLUE	14	18
7	PURPLE	10	8
8	MAGENTA	6	2
9	BLACK OUTLINE	2	0

over 1/2 done ← WOW!

Point out that after learning what's on the first 4 Wrap-ups they are over half done.

It has been stated that we remember:[*]

"20% of what we read, 30% of what we hear,
40% of what we see,   50% of what we say, 60% of what we do
and _90% of what we see, hear, say and do_."

* Accelerated Learning Action Guide by Brian Tracy, with Colin Rose.

The Learning Wrap-ups System for learning is called "SEE, SAY, WRAP-UP, WRITE" and the "HEAR" is incorporated with the use of the "WRAP-UP RAP" audio cassette.

SECRET 4

SINGING AND SAYING IT WITH THE "WRAP-UP RAP"

Old and young alike enjoy talking along with the rhythm of the cassette tape. The tape presents each set of problems twice: first, the problems with answers; and second, the problems without answers. Then after each set of numbers has been completed, it goes through all of the number facts a third time at mastery level speed. Facts are presented in the same order as found on the Learning Wrap-up. There are 2 tapes, 1 for addition, 1 for subtraction. When students can use the Wrap-up, it is fun to do it with the audio tape.

"Grab your WRAP-UPS

and get your string...

We're gonna' do

that Wrap-up thing.

Add 4, here we go...

We're doing the Wrap-up, the Wrap-up Rap!"

SECRET 5
LEARNING NEW CONCEPTS WITH THE "1," "2," "3" FACTS

Each of us has a certain amount of mental capacity that can be used at one time. It is easier for students to learn a new idea, concept or method for solving a problem with numbers they already know all the answers for. Then they can concentrate on the concept. Later, when they are learning to find answers for "bigger" numbers, they do not have to be concerned about doing the problem the correct way. Providing for very early successful experiences helps the student to have a positive attitude about math and an eagerness to learn more.

SECRET 6
SOLVING PROBLEMS THAT ARE "ABOUT ME"

Word problems are printed with a space for the students to write in their own names, the names of their friends or family.

Problems are basically written so that they could actually have happened to the students in the classroom or at home with their families. To help students relate to the problems, the teacher can actually set up some of the "About Me" situations in the classroom. Write in the names of the students, or let them choose a name they would like to put with each problem.

The teacher should read the problems aloud, and talk about them as a class. This gives students the opportunity to enjoy the word problems together. Make certain every student's name gets used if you are writing them in. Have students create some word problem situations. Then set up the problems and work them together on the chalkboard while they write the problems on their paper or individual lap boards. Photocopy a page of the students' problems and let the whole class do them.

SAMPLE

In class we "TALKED ABOUT PETS."
We kept a chart showing all of the pets, then wrote math problems. We knew that if we could solve the original problem, we could do at least 3 more problems using the same numbers.

1. _____ counted the students who had dogs for pets. There were 8. 6 students had cats. What was the total number of dogs and cats?

2. _____ said she had a stuffed giraffe and a stuffed elephant for her pets. _____ had 6 teddy bears. How many stuffed animals did the two of them have?

3. _____had 8 goldfish, but the cat ate 2 of them. How many were left? Can you do the commutative partners and subtraction buddy to go with this problem?

4. _____, _____ and _____ said they didn't have pets, but each drew a picture of the pet they would like to have. _____ said he had pictures of 6 horses he would like to own if he could. What was the total number of animal pictures?

SECRET 7

FACT FAMILY SHEETS for 1's. It becomes very clear to the students that once they know a fact, they really know 4 facts. The FAMILY FACT SHEETS are presented clearly and ask the students to use what they know to extend their knowledge by use of commutative partners and inverse operations. **"Commutative Partners"/"Subtraction Buddies"** cards can be used for games and activities as well as drill in and out of the classroom.

The FACT FAMILY SHEETS format is then used for 1's, 10's and 100's to increase under-standing of place value while memorizing the facts. Students learn that if they can add pennies in the 1's column, they can use what they know to add dimes in the 10's column, and dollars in the 100's column. There are several worksheets to give them practice with this concept.

FACT FAMILIES

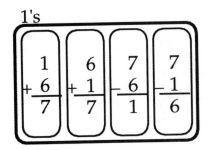

1's

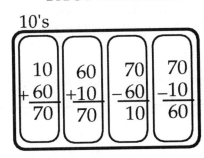

10's   100's

Then use the KEY to unlocking their hidden knowledge with   **"I KNOW...SO..."**

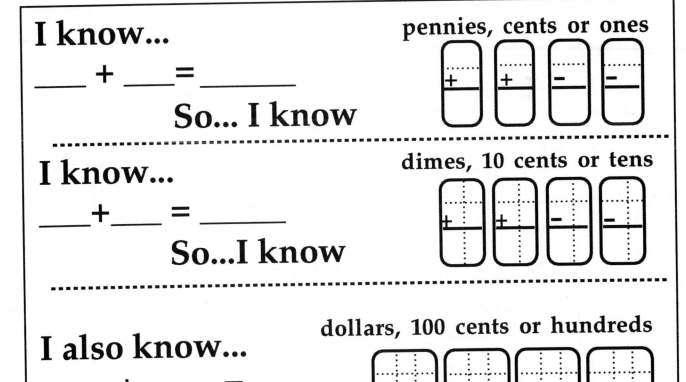

© Learning Wrap-ups Inc. 1997

SECRET 8

USING THE "POWER PAGE"

Once students understand "I KNOW... SO" (the place value and inverse operation), they learn that if they know just 1 fact, (Example: 3 + 2 = 5) there are at least 52 problems they can do, using numbers with only 3 digits or less. They soon begin to realize the power they will have when they master all add/subtract facts.

SAMPLE

I know that 3 + 4 = 7
Therefore, I know...

$\frac{3}{+4} \quad \frac{4}{+3} \quad \frac{7}{-3} \quad \frac{7}{-4}$
$\overline{7} \quad \overline{7} \quad \overline{4} \quad \overline{3}$

and I can do all of these problems!!!

3	4	30	40	33	44	34	43	300	400	330	440	303
+4	+3	+40	+30	+44	+33	+43	+34	+400	+300	+440	+330	+404

404	403	304	340	430	333	444	334	443	343	434	433	344
+303	+304	+403	+430	+340	+444	+333	+443	+334	+434	+343	+344	+433

7	7	70	70	77	77	77	77	700	700	770	770	707
-4	-3	-40	-30	-44	-33	-43	-34	-400	-300	-440	-330	-404

707	707	707	770	770	777	777	777	777	777	777	777	777
-303	-403	-304	-340	-430	-333	-444	-443	-334	-434	-343	-344	-433

POWER PAGE 3 + 4 = 7

At first, use facts with 1-digit answers. Later, use the "Student Blank Power Page" to write problems with regrouping.

←

Give students a fact and have them write all the problems they can think of.

↓

SAMPLE

I KNOW__ + __ = ___ SO....
I can write and answer this many problems.

A.

B.

C.

This page will help students learn alignment and also includes space for regrouping when necessary.

STUDENT POWER PAGE

SECRET 9

BECOMING FRIENDS WITH THE "REGROUPING PAIRS" p. 30.   Any pair of numbers that call for regrouping fits into these catagories. This program teaches about numbers that are important to know. We have to make a special effort to understand, use and be friends with them. It pays big dividends. We can start teaching "regrouping" as soon as we use pennies to add 1 + 9. Why would 1+ 9 need "REGROUPING" when 10 + 9 does not? A little detective work with the students turns this into a fun concept.

See the regrouping instructions on pp. 67, 68.
A blank regrouping page for writing problems can be found on p. 28.

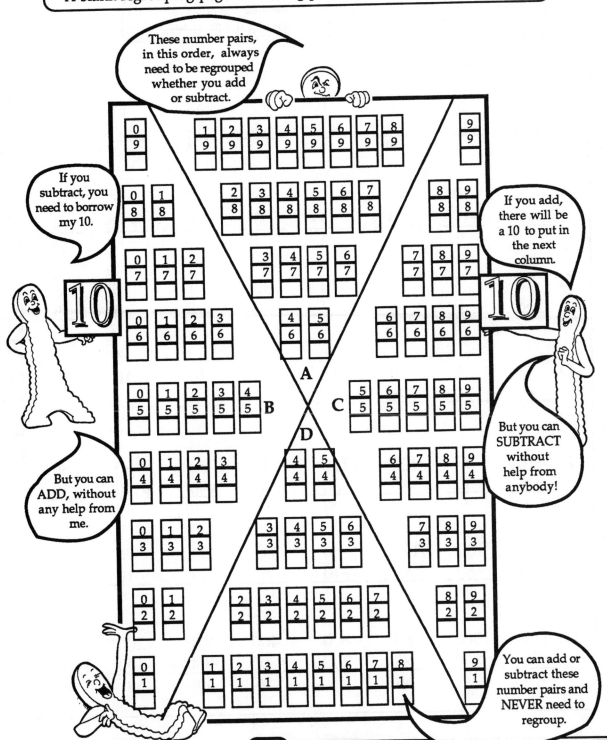

© Learning Wrap-ups Inc. 1997

SECRET 10

CHALLENGING A "THINKER SHEET" Students pair off to practice the ADD and SUBTRACT facts mentally. Super easy facts get them going early and provide success immediately.   With each set of numbers, the regrouping pairs will get a little extra attention. Students should know the regrouping pairs so well they do not have to think about it.

SAMPLE

> Two students work together. One reads the problems, the other gives the answers from memory. Take turns reading the problems.

Watch the signs!

+ - 8 THINKER SHEET

A.
11	20	8	0	12	16	11	8
-8	-12	+2	+8	+8	-8	-3	-6
3	8	10	8	20	8	8	2

B.
8	19	14	15	8	17	8	8
+8	-11	-8	-7	-7	-8	+11	-4
16	8	6	8	1	9	19	4

C.
15	8	7	10	13	1	8	8
-8	-0	+8	-2	-5	+8	+4	+5
7	8	15	8	8	9	12	13

D.
3	5	19	18	8	10	10	8
+8	+8	-8	-10	+7	-8	+8	-5
11	13	11	8	15	2	18	3

E.
80	80	120	160	80	80	80	80
-10	+80	-80	-80	+30	+90	+120	-30
70	160	40	80	110	170	200	50

F.
110	180	170	80	60	80	90	80
+80	-80	-90	+10	+80	-80	-10	+60
190	100	80	90	140	00	80	140

G.
900	1300	1400	800	400	900	1200	800
+800	-800	- 600	-200	+800	-800	-400	+1000
1700	500	800	600	1200	100	800	1800

WORKING WITH OLDER STUDENTS

This program can be used very successfully with students who:
- should but don't already know their addition and subtraction facts.
- do not yet fully understand the relationship between add and subtract.
- need to start solving problems mentally.

Older students (generally from 3rd grade on, including adults) respond well and learn very quickly using LEARNING WRAP-UPS. They like competition, and will practice hard to beat the stop watch. Set goals of 40, 30 and 20 seconds, then have them set their own goals. When they have memorized each of the 10 sets of facts on the Wrap-ups, all the other work becomes increasingly easier.

Most of the work in this book can be done mentally. Give each pair of students one page of **problems without answers and one page with answers for correcting. Have them practice figuring the answers mentally, then saying them aloud. Then switch papers and the second student gives the answers. Most of our everyday math is done mentally. Prepare your students.** Have students time themselves with every assignment they do. Tell them that timing themselves is a good way to assess their own progress. Be sure they understand, however, that <u>accuracy</u> is most important.

It is recommended that students do each of the worksheets. However, if there are more things to do with + - 1 and 2 than you feel are necessary, move on but come back to the + - 1 when you start using a new concept for a higher number. It will help the students understand what is wanted from them when they are not concerned about the higher numbers. Then they can go back to higher numbers and not have to worry about the format or concept.

It is essential that students:

1. **Can count forward and backward.** Use whatever materials that are needed, to insure this skill is mastered.

2. **Understand the place value of dollars, dimes and pennies.** It adapts to place value quickly.

3. **Know how to use a Learning Wrap-up,** which they will do for longer periods of time.

4. **Take frequent breaks** and use alternate activities (singing, writing along with the Wrap-up Rap, calling out answers, writing on a lap board, etc.)

5. <u>**Understand how much they know.**</u> Use the charts. (The commutative property of addition and the inverse operation of subtraction.) Keep stressing that with this system, once they learn one addition fact, they literally can do dozens of problems. They actually know not only 4 facts on the add-subtract chart, but they can apply that knowledge to those same numbers in the 10's, 100's, and 1000's columns. POWER PAGES let them see literally how much they know, when they know just one fact.

6. **Start thinking mentally to find answers.** Frequent opportunities to stretch their mental powers must be provided. **THINKER SHEETS** are provided for students to review mentally the facts learned each day. **POWER PAGES** can also provide opportunities to do mental math.

The **POWER PAGES** give the students more opportunities to mentally add and subtract up to 3-digit numbers. Use these pages as you would a THINKER SHEET. Have students write Power Pages of their own with digits totaling less than 9. Tell them to think the problems from left to right. Later, they use Power Pages with REGROUPING PAIRS, and think the answers mentally.

Give them ample opportunity to spot and manage regrouping number combinations.

BEFORE YOU BEGIN THE PROGRAM:

- Each student should each have:

    A folder in which he or she can put daily assignments, daily records and Learning Charts.

    A paper cup or bag with 20 pennies, and/or other substitute money.

    A set of Addition Learning Wrap-ups and

    A set of Subtraction Learning Wrap-ups.

    Colored pencils (preferred) or crayons.

- The teacher should have:

    A stop watch to be used with older students who may be in this program. (Be cautious about using the stop watch with younger children.)

    The work pages as needed for each set of numbers.

    The WRAP-UP RAP audio tapes for Addition and Subtraction.

- You will find the 10 SECRETS and support material to help students learn with each of the sets of addition and subtraction facts 1 through 10. Because each Learning Wrap-up board goes to 12, we have included the 12's in some of the written work. Students using Learning Wrap-ups learn through their 12's quickly. Because ours is a country that uses dozens, gross, and base 12 with time and measurement it was decided it would be worthwhile to include the 11's and 12's in this program. Learning Wrap-ups do not teach the "0" facts or 11-11, 11-12, or 12-12 combinations. Make certain students understand them, and that if they know 1's, 2's, and 10's, they can do all of the facts.

TO HEIGHTEN INTEREST:

> "We remember best what is at the first and at the last of a session." *

These suggestions are to be used at the teacher's discretion, but use them frequently. Do something different every day. Keep students guessing and excited.

- Take frequent breaks, or change the activity.
- Try CHECKING PROGRESS activities first thing in the morning.
- Sing and dance to the Wrap-up Rap.
- Just before recess do the Wrap-ups.
- Have students sit on the floor and place their writing paper on the chair seat.
- Do Wrap-ups while sitting <u>on</u> their desks.
- Let students sit on the floor back to back.
- Play musical chairs. (Place unwrapped Wrap-ups on chairs.) Students walk around. When the music stops, students wrap and then sit. No one is left without a seat, but students always try to get an easy Wrap-up and don't want to be the last to sit down.
- Invite the principal to come see how well your students are doing. Send your students to the office to get some praise.
- Group by row, table, hair color, birthday months, number of letters in names, height, color of shoes, Velcro or laces, buttons on clothing to do their Wrap-ups or worksheets.
- MOST IMPORTANT!! Let students develop some of the activities they think will help them learn. They usually have great ideas. After all, this program is for them. They will give it everything they have, if they are part of the planning.

* Accelerated Learning Action Guide by Brian Tracy, with Colin Rose.

SECTION II

INFORMATION TO PHOTOCOPY

FOR USE WITH STUDENTS

TEACHER'S CHOICE

1 The Web Sight Addition/Subtraction sheet is not referred to in the lesson plans, but is included here for a variety of drill and practice needs.
2 The Ordered Add/Subtract Facts sheet is useful for pointing out commutative property, showing patterns and developing a sense of using doubles to build upon.
3 Number Combinations Chart can be used to help students develop confidence in adding mentally with regrouping from left to right.
4 Mathnique Money can be used for letting students know that YOU KNOW they are working to accomplish specific goals. Suggestions for spending: Good as new items, field trips, extra recess time, merchants' donations, etc.

MATHNIQUE COLORING CHART

HERE'S WHAT I'VE LEARNED

NAME _____ # _____

	1	2	3	4	5	6	7	8	9	10	11	12
1	1+1=2 2-1=1	1+2=3 3-2=1	1+3=4 4-3=1	1+4=5 5-4=1	1+5=6 6-5=1	1+6=7 7-6=1	1+7=8 8-7=1	1+8=9 9-8=1	1+9=10 10-9=1	1+10=11 11-10=1	1+11=12 12-11=1	1+12=13 13-12=1
2	2+1=3 3-1=2	2+2=4 4-2=2	2+3=5 5-3=2	2+4=6 6-4=2	2+5=7 7-5=2	2+6=8 8-6=2	2+7=9 9-7=2	2+8=10 10-8=2	2+9=11 11-9=2	2+10=12 12-10=2	2+11=13 13-11=2	2+12=14 14-12=2
3	3+1=4 4-1=3	3+2=5 5-2=3	3+3=6 6-3=3	3+4=7 7-4=3	3+5=8 8-5=3	3+6=9 9-6=3	3+7=10 10-7=3	3+8=11 11-8=3	3+9=12 12-9=3	3+10=13 13-10=3	3+11=14 14-11=3	3+12=15 15-12=3
4	4+1=5 5-1=4	4+2=6 6-2=4	4+3=7 7-3=4	4+4=8 8-4=4	4+5=9 9-5=4	4+6=10 10-6=4	4+7=11 11-7=4	4+8=12 12-8=4	4+9=13 13-9=4	4+10=14 14-10=4	4+11=15 15-11=4	4+12=16 16-12=4
5	5+1=6 6-1=5	5+2=7 7-2=5	5+3=8 8-3=5	5+4=9 9-4=5	5+5=10 10-5=5	5+6=11 11-6=5	5+7=12 12-7=5	5+8=13 13-8=5	5+9=14 14-9=5	5+10=15 15-10=5	5+11=16 16-11=5	5+12=17 17-12=5
6	6+1=7 7-1=6	6+2=8 8-2=6	6+3=9 9-3=6	6+4=10 10-4=6	6+5=11 11-5=6	6+6=12 12-6=6	6+7=13 13-7=6	6+8=14 14-8=6	6+9=15 15-9=6	6+10=16 16-10=6	6+11=17 17-11=6	6+12=18 18-12=6
7	7+1=8 8-1=7	7+2=9 9-2=7	7+3=10 10-3=7	7+4=11 11-4=7	7+5=12 12-5=7	7+6=13 13-6=7	7+7=14 14-7=7	7+8=15 15-8=7	7+9=16 16-9=7	7+10=17 17-10=7	7+11=18 18-11=7	7+12=19 19-12=7
8	8+1=9 9-1=8	8+2=10 10-2=8	8+3=11 11-3=8	8+4=12 12-4=8	8+5=13 13-5=8	8+6=14 14-6=8	8+7=15 15-7=8	8+8=16 16-8=8	8+9=17 17-9=8	8+10=18 18-10=8	8+11=19 19-11=8	8+12=20 20-12=8
9	9+1=10 10-1=9	9+2=11 11-2=9	9+3=12 12-3=9	9+4=13 13-4=9	9+5=14 14-5=9	9+6=15 15-6=9	9+7=16 16-7=9	9+8=17 17-8=9	9+9=18 18-9=9	9+10=19 19-10=9	9+11=20 20-11=9	9+12=21 21-12=9
10	10+1=11 11-1=10	10+2=12 12-2=10	10+3=13 13-3=10	10+4=14 14-4=10	10+5=15 15-5=10	10+6=16 16-6=10	10+7=17 17-7=10	10+8=18 18-8=10	10+9=19 19-9=10	10+10=20 20-10=10	10+11=21 21-11=10	10+12=20 20-12=10
11	11+1=12 12-1=11	11+2=13 13-2=11	11+3=14 14-3=11	11+4=15 15-4=11	11+5=16 16-5=11	11+6=17 17-6=11	11+7=18 18-7=11	11+8=19 19-8=11	11+9=20 20-9=11	11+10=21 21-10=11	11+11=22 22-11=11	11+12=23 23-12=11
12	12+1=13 13-1=12	12+2=14 14-2=12	12+3=15 15-3=12	12+4=16 16-4=12	12+5=17 17-5=12	12+6=18 18-6=12	12+7=19 19-7=12	12+8=20 20-8=12	12+9=21 21-9=12	12+10=22 22-10=12	12+11=23 23-11=12	12+12=24 24-12=12

Print 2 copies for each student. (1 to take home, 1 for school)

 © Learning Wrap-ups Inc. 1997

TRACK YOUR PROGRESS

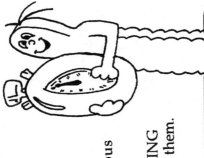

Start at the bottom and fill in a square above the numbered WRAP-UP you are using, every time you complete the WRAP-UP correctly. Do it over and over. Mark a square each time. The more you wrap, the higher you climb, and the better you know your facts.

A favorite slogan......

Good, Better, Best,
Never let it rest,
'Till the Good gets Better
and the Better gets Best!

--Anonymous

Set some WRITING or WRAPPING goals, then see if you can reach them.

Reaching Goals

	1	2	3	4	5	6	7	8	9	10	
											Next to impossible!
											Incredible!
											Super Champ!
											Champion!
											First Goal Keep it up!
											Good work! You're Learning!
											You're getting acquainted

Keeping Track

1	2	3	4	5	6	7	8	9	10

© Learning Wrap-ups Inc. 1997

Print 2 copies per student. 1 to take home, 1 for school.

100 CIRCLES, ALL PURPOSE COUNTING CHART Use for 1's, 5's, 10's, 25's or 100's

(THOUSANDS)	(HUNDREDS) 100's	(TENS) 10's	(ONES) 1's
1000's	Take dollars off and put a marker in the 1000's column	Take dimes off and put a dollar in the 100's column	Take pennies off and put a dime in the 10's column
10,000 TRADE	1000 TRADE	100 TRADE	10 TRADE
9000	900	90	9
8000	800	80	8
7000	700	70	7
6000	600	60	6
5000	500	50	5
4000	400	40	4
3000	300	30	3
2000	200	20	2
1000	100	10	1
	DOLLARS	DIMES	PENNIES

DOLLAR, DIME & PENNY CHART

Cut dollar section away, and color both sides of paper green. Then cut into separate dollar pieces.

dollar 100	dollar 100
dollar 100	dollar 100
dollar 100	dollar 100
dollar 100	dollar 100
dollar 100	dollar 100
dollar 100	dollar 100
dollar 100	dollar 100
dollar 100	dollar 100
dollar 100	dollar 100
dollar 100	dollar 100
dollar 100	dollar 100
dollar 100	dollar 100
dollar 100	dollar 100
dollar 100	dollar 100
dollar 100	dollar 100

Leave white and cut out coins.

dime 10	dime 10	dime 10
dime 10	dime 10	dime 10
dime 10	dime 10	dime 10
dime 10	dime 10	dime 10
dime 10	dime 10	dime 10
dime 10	dime 10	dime 10
dime 10	dime 10	dime 10
dime 10	dime 10	dime 10
dime 10	dime 10	dime 10
dime 10	dime 10	dime 10

Cut penny section away, and color both sides of paper brown. Then cut into separate penny pieces.

penny 1	penny 1	penny 1
penny 1	penny 1	penny 1
penny 1	penny 1	penny 1
penny 1	penny 1	penny 1
penny 1	penny 1	penny 1
penny 1	penny 1	penny 1
penny 1	penny 1	penny 1
penny 1	penny 1	penny 1
penny 1	penny 1	penny 1
penny 1	penny 1	penny 1

Color both sides gold and cut out.

1000	1000	1000	1000	1000	1000	1000

ADD

$1+1=$ ___	$2+2=$ ___	$3+3=$ ___	$4+4=$ ___	$12+5=$ ___
$3+1=$ ___	$5+2=$ ___	$7+3=$ ___	$6+4=$ ___	$10+5=$ ___
$9+1=$ ___	$12+2=$ ___	$11+3=$ ___	$8+4=$ ___	$7+5=$ ___
$6+1=$ ___	$1+2=$ ___	$5+3=$ ___	$11+4=$ ___	$5+5=$ ___
$10+1=$ ___	$9+2=$ ___	$8+3=$ ___	$1+4=$ ___	$4+5=$ ___
$2+1=$ ___	$6+2=$ ___	$4+3=$ ___	$9+4=$ ___	$9+5=$ ___
$11+1=$ ___	$10+2=$ ___	$6+3=$ ___	$3+4=$ ___	$8+5=$ ___
$4+1=$ ___	$8+2=$ ___	$2+3=$ ___	$12+4=$ ___	$6+5=$ ___
$8+1=$ ___	$11+2=$ ___	$12+3=$ ___	$2+4=$ ___	$3+5=$ ___
$12+1=$ ___	$3+2=$ ___	$1+3=$ ___	$10+4=$ ___	$2+5=$ ___
$7+1=$ ___	$7+2=$ ___	$9+3=$ ___	$5+4=$ ___	$11+5=$ ___
$5+1=$ ___	$4+2=$ ___	$10+3=$ ___	$7+4=$ ___	$1+5=$ ___

SUBTRACT

$2-1=$ ___	$8-2=$ ___	$4-3=$ ___	$16-4=$ ___	$7-5=$ ___
$4-1=$ ___	$13-2=$ ___	$7-3=$ ___	$10-4=$ ___	$17-5=$ ___
$10-1=$ ___	$7-2=$ ___	$15-3=$ ___	$15-4=$ ___	$12-5=$ ___
$7-1=$ ___	$4-2=$ ___	$12-3=$ ___	$7-4=$ ___	$6-5=$ ___
$8-1=$ ___	$14-2=$ ___	$11-3=$ ___	$13-4=$ ___	$15-5=$ ___
$5-1=$ ___	$3-2=$ ___	$14-3=$ ___	$8-4=$ ___	$10-5=$ ___
$11-1=$ ___	$12-2=$ ___	$6-3=$ ___	$6-4=$ ___	$14-5=$ ___
$3-1=$ ___	$5-2=$ ___	$9-3=$ ___	$14-4=$ ___	$16-5=$ ___
$12-1=$ ___	$10-2=$ ___	$10-3=$ ___	$5-4=$ ___	$9-5=$ ___
$13-1=$ ___	$6-2=$ ___	$13-3=$ ___	$11-4=$ ___	$13-5=$ ___
$9-1=$ ___	$11-2=$ ___	$8-3=$ ___	$9-4=$ ___	$11-5=$ ___
$6-1=$ ___	$9-2=$ ___	$5-3=$ ___	$12-4=$ ___	$8-5=$ ___

23

+ -PRE/POST TEST 6-10 FACTS   NAME   #

ADD

1+6=	7+7=	1+8=	6+9=	6+10=
5+6=	1+7=	7+8=	1+9=	1+10=
2+6=	3+7=	12+8=	12+9=	12+10=
12+6=	6+7=	4+8=	5+9=	2+10=
8+6=	9+7=	2+8=	9+9=	8+10=
11+6=	2+7=	6+8=	2+9=	9+10=
9+6=	12+7=	3+8=	11+9=	5+10=
6+6=	11+7=	10+8=	4+9=	3+10=
4+6=	5+7=	11+8=	10+9=	4+10=
10+6=	8+7=	8+8=	7+9=	11+10=
3+6=	4+7=	9+8=	3+9=	7+10=
7+6=	10+7=	5+8=	8+9=	10+10=

+ -PRE/POST TEST 6-10 FACTS   NAME   #

SUBTRACT

18-6=	17-7=	12-8=	20-9=	17-10=
13-6=	8-7=	20-8=	10-9=	22-10=
9-6=	19-7=	11-8=	21-9=	11-10=
15-6=	15-7=	13-8=	19-9=	14-10=
10-6=	9-7=	15-8=	11-9=	20-10=
17-6=	10-7=	14-8=	18-9=	15-10=
7-6=	11-7=	9-8=	13-9=	21-10=
16-6=	14-7=	17-8=	16-9=	16-10=
11-6=	18-7=	10-8=	17-9=	13-10=
12-6=	13-7=	16-8=	14-9=	18-10=
14-6=	16-7=	19-8=	12-9=	12-10=
8-6=	12-7=	18-8=	15-9=	19-10=

24

#3 FACTS

3+8= ___	7-3= ___
3+1= ___	15-3= ___
3+3= ___	6-3= ___
3+5= ___	12-3= ___
3+12= ___	4-3= ___
3+10= ___	11-3= ___
3+2= ___	10-3= ___
3+6= ___	8-3= ___
3+4= ___	14-3= ___
3+9= ___	13-3= ___
3+11= ___	9-3= ___
3+7= ___	5-3= ___
time ___	time ___

#2 FACTS

2+3= ___	9-2= ___
2+7= ___	10-2= ___
2+1= ___	3-2= ___
2+12= ___	11-2= ___
2+5= ___	5-2= ___
2+10= ___	4-2= ___
2+4= ___	14-2= ___
2+8= ___	12-2= ___
2+11= ___	13-2= ___
2+2= ___	7-2= ___
2+6= ___	6-2= ___
2+9= ___	8-2= ___
time ___	time ___

#1 FACTS

1+1= ___	6-1= ___
1+8= ___	8-1= ___
1+5= ___	11-1= ___
1+2= ___	2-1= ___
1+10= ___	10-1= ___
1+7= ___	3-1= ___
1+9= ___	5-1= ___
1+3= ___	7-1= ___
1+11= ___	13-1= ___
1+6= ___	9-1= ___
1+12= ___	12-1= ___
1+4= ___	4-1= ___
time ___	time ___

#4 FACTS

4+1= _____   6-4= _____
4+8= _____   8-4= _____
4+5= _____   11-4= _____
4+2= _____   14-4= _____
4+10= _____   10-4= _____
4+7= _____   15-4= _____
4+9= _____   5-4= _____
4+3= _____   7-4= _____
4+11= _____   13-4= _____
4+6= _____   9-4= _____
4+12= _____   12-4= _____
4+4= _____   16-4= _____

time _____

#5 FACTS

5+3= _____   9-5= _____
5+7= _____   10-5= _____
5+1= _____   15-5= _____
5+12= _____   11-5= _____
5+5= _____   16-5= _____
5+10= _____   17-5= _____
5+4= _____   14-5= _____
5+8= _____   12-5= _____
5+11= _____   13-5= _____
5+2= _____   7-5= _____
5+6= _____   6-5= _____
5+9= _____   8-5= _____

time _____

#6 FACTS

6+8= _____   7-6= _____
6+1= _____   15-6= _____
6+3= _____   16-6= _____
6+5= _____   12-6= _____
6+12= _____   17-6= _____
6+10= _____   11-6= _____
6+2= _____   10-6= _____
6+6= _____   8-6= _____
6+4= _____   14-6= _____
6+9= _____   13-6= _____
6+11= _____   9-6= _____
6+7= _____   18-6= _____

time _____

#7 FACTS
QUICK QUIZ   NAME   #

7+1= ___	17-7= ___
7+8= ___	8-7= ___
7+5= ___	11-7= ___
7+2= ___	14-7= ___
7+10= ___	10-7= ___
7+7= ___	15-7= ___
7+9= ___	18-7= ___
7+3= ___	19-7= ___
7+11= ___	13-7= ___
7+6= ___	9-7= ___
7+12= ___	12-7= ___
7+4= ___	16-7= ___
time ___	time ___

#8 FACTS
QUICK QUIZ   NAME   #

8+3= ___	9-8= ___
8+7= ___	10-8= ___
8+1= ___	20-8= ___
8+12= ___	11-8= ___
8+5= ___	16-8= ___
8+10= ___	15-8= ___
8+4= ___	14-8= ___
8+8= ___	12-8= ___
8+11= ___	13-8= ___
8+2= ___	19-8= ___
8+6= ___	17-8= ___
8+9= ___	18-8= ___
time ___	time ___

#9 FACTS
QUICK QUIZ   NAME   #

9+8= ___	20-9= ___
9+1= ___	15-9= ___
9+3= ___	16-9= ___
9+5= ___	12-9= ___
9+12= ___	17-9= ___
9+10= ___	11-9= ___
9+2= ___	10-9= ___
9+6= ___	19-9= ___
9+4= ___	14-9= ___
9+9= ___	13-9= ___
9+11= ___	21-9= ___
9+7= ___	18-9= ___
time ___	time ___

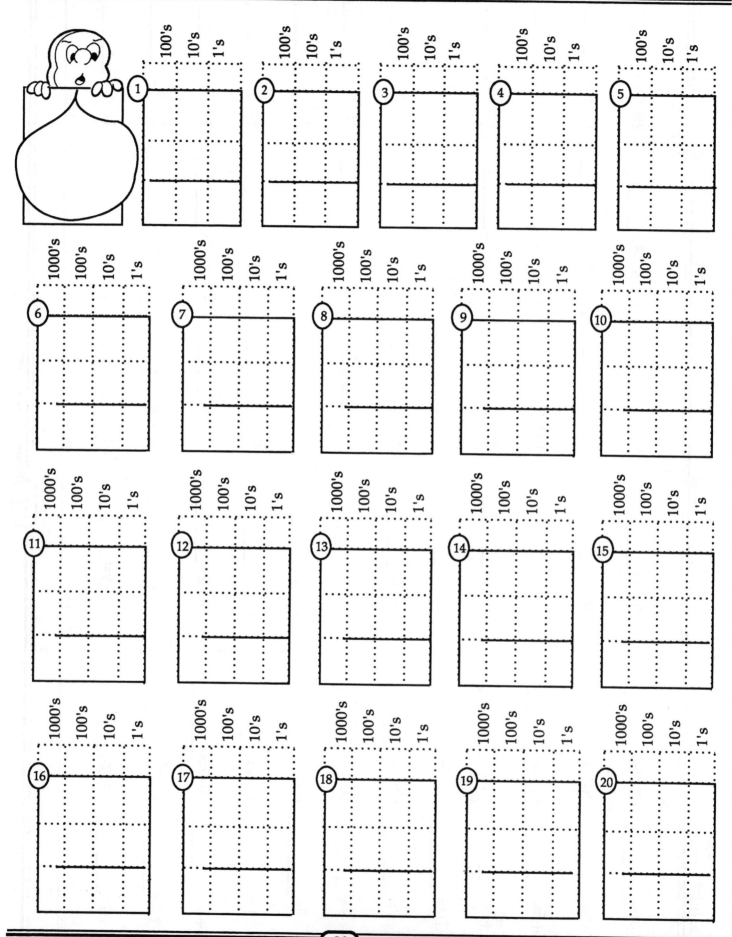

NAME #

STUDENT POWER PAGE

I KNOW__ + __ = ___ SO... I CAN WRITE AND ANSWER THIS MANY PROBLEMS.

A.

1's +

1's +

10's 1's +

10's 1's +

10's 1's +

10's 1's +

10's 1's +

100's 10's 1's +

100's 10's 1's +

100's 10's 1's +

B.

1's −

1's −

10's 1's −

10's 1's −

10's 1's −

10's 1's −

10's 1's −

100's 10's 1's −

100's 10's 1's −

100's 10's 1's −

C.

100's 10's 1's

100's 10's 1's

100's 10's 1's

100's 10's 1's

100's 10's 1's

100's 10's 1's

100's 10's 1's

1. Write a page with facts that have a 1-digit answer. 2. Write problems with regrouping.
This page can be used later as a THINKER SHEET for Mental Math. One paper has the problems only. The other has problems and answers. Two students work together. One says the problem, ie, " two hundred and twenty two plus one hundred and eleven." The other student mentally computes and gives the answer. They then trade papers.

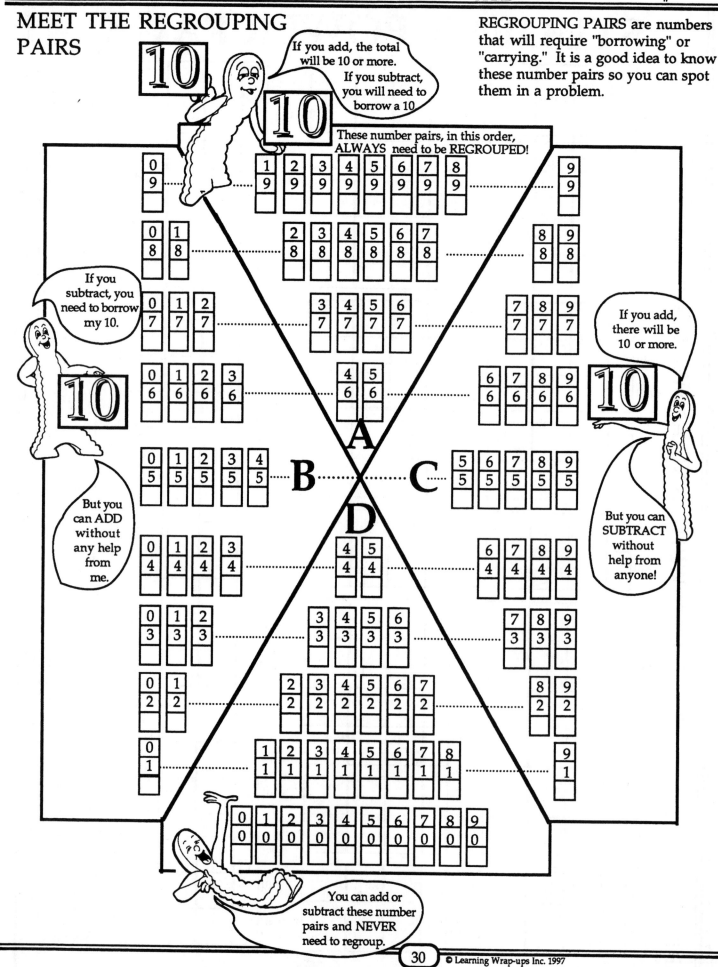

WEB SIGHT ADDITION OR SUBTRACTION   NAME _____   #_____ DATE _____

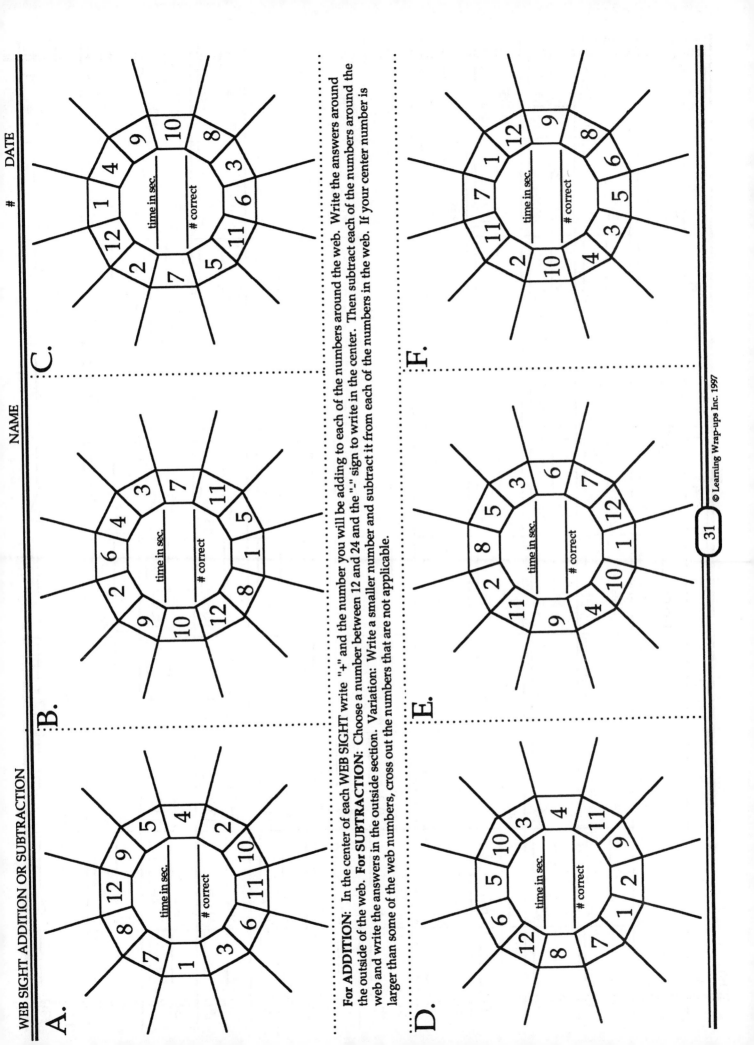

A.
(web with numbers: 12, 9, 5, 4, 2, 8, 7, 1, 3, 6, 11, 10)
time in sec. _____
correct _____

B.
(web with numbers: 2, 6, 4, 3, 7, 11, 5, 1, 8, 12, 10, 9)
time in sec. _____
correct _____

C.
(web with numbers: 4, 9, 10, 1, 8, 12, 3, 2, 6, 7, 5, 11)
time in sec. _____
correct _____

For **ADDITION:** In the center of each WEB SIGHT write "+" and the number you will be adding to each of the numbers around the web. Write the answers around the outside of the web. For **SUBTRACTION:** Choose a number between 12 and 24 and the "-" sign to write in the center. Then subtract each of the numbers around the web and write the answers in the outside section. **Variation:** Write a smaller number and subtract it from each of the numbers in the web. If your center number is larger than some of the web numbers, cross out the numbers that are not applicable.

D.
(web with numbers: 10, 3, 4, 5, 11, 6, 9, 12, 7, 1, 2, 8)
time in sec. _____
correct _____

E.
(web with numbers: 5, 3, 6, 8, 7, 2, 12, 11, 1, 9, 4, 10)
time in sec. _____
correct _____

F.
(web with numbers: 1, 12, 9, 7, 8, 11, 6, 2, 5, 10, 3, 4)
time in sec. _____
correct _____

+ – ORDERED FACTS Use for showing patterns, teaching doubles, building on doubles, etc.

1	2	3	4	5	6	7	8	9	10
1+1= 2-1=	1+2= 3-2=	1+3= 4-3=	1+4= 5-4=	1+5= 6-5=	1+6= 7-6=	1+7= 8-7=	1+8= 9-8=	1+9= 10-9=	1+10= 11-10=
2+1= 3-1=	2+2= 4-2=	2+3= 5-3=	2+4= 6-4=	2+5= 7-5=	2+6= 8-6=	2+7= 9-7=	2+8= 10-8=	2+9= 11-9=	2+10= 12-10=
3+1= 4-1=	3+2= 5-2=	3+3= 6-3=	3+4= 7-4=	3+5= 8-5=	3+6= 9-6=	3+7= 10-7=	3+8= 11-8=	3+9= 12-9=	3+10= 13-10=
4+1= 5-1=	4+2= 6-2=	4+3= 7-3=	4+4= 8-4=	4+5= 9-5=	4+6= 10-6=	4+7= 11-7=	4+8= 12-8=	4+9= 13-9=	4+10= 14-10=
5+1= 6-1=	5+2= 7-2=	5+3= 8-3=	5+4= 9-4=	5+5= 10-5=	5+6= 11-6=	5+7= 12-7=	5+8= 13-8=	5+9= 14-9=	5+10= 15-10=
6+1= 7-1=	6+2= 8-2=	6+3= 9-3=	6+4= 10-4=	6+5= 11-5=	6+6= 12-6=	6+7= 13-7=	6+8= 14-8=	6+9= 15-9=	6+10= 16-10=
7+1= 8-1=	7+2= 9-2=	7+3= 10-3=	7+4= 11-4=	7+5= 12-5=	7+6= 13-6=	7+7= 14-7=	7+8= 15-8=	7+9= 16-9=	7+10= 17-10=
8+1= 9-1=	8+2= 10-2=	8+3= 11-3=	8+4= 12-4=	8+5= 13-5=	8+6= 14-6=	8+7= 15-7=	8+8= 16-8=	8+9= 17-9=	8+10= 18-10=
9+1= 10-1=	9+2= 11-2=	9+3= 12-3=	9+4= 13-4=	9+5= 14-5=	9+6= 15-6=	9+7= 16-7=	9+8= 17-8=	9+9= 18-9=	9+10= 19-10=
10+1= 11-1=	10+2= 12-2=	10+3= 13-3=	10+4= 14-4=	10+5= 15-5=	10+6= 16-6=	10+7= 17-7=	10+8= 18-8=	10+9= 19-9=	10+10= 20-10=
11+1= 12-1=	11+2= 13-2=	11+3= 14-3=	11+4= 15-4=	11+5= 16-5=	11+6= 17-6=	11+7= 18-7=	11+8= 19-8=	11+9= 20-9=	11+10= 21-10=
12+1= 13-1=	12+2= 14-2=	12+3= 15-3=	12+4= 16-4=	12+5= 17-5=	12+6= 18-6=	12+7= 19-7=	12+8= 20-8=	12+9= 21-9=	12+10= 22-10=

32

1-digit **addititon** addend combinations that put a specific number in the ones column of the sum. This is helpful to the person who does addition mentally with regrouping from left to right.

1-digit sums

0
0

What addends combine to put a 0 in the ones column?

2-digit sums

1	2	3	4	5
9	8	7	6	5

1-digit sums

1
0

What addends combine to put a 1 in the ones column?

2-digit sums

2	3	4	5
9	8	7	6

1-digit sums

2	1
0	1

What addends combine to put a 2 in the ones column?

2-digit sums

3	4	5	6
9	8	7	6

1-digit sums

3	2
0	1

What addends combine to put a 3 in the ones column?

2-digit sums

4	5	6
9	8	7

1-digit sums

4	3	2
0	1	2

What addends combine to put a 4 in the ones column?

2-digit sums

5	6	7
9	8	7

1-digit sums

5	4	3
0	1	2

What addends combine to put a 5 in the ones column?

2-digit sums

6	7
9	8

1-digit sums

6	5	4	3
0	1	2	3

What addends combine to put a 6 in the ones column?

2-digit sums

7	8
9	8

1-digit sums

7	6	5	4
0	1	2	3

What addends combine to put a 7 in the ones column?

2-digit sums

8
9

1-digit sums

8	7	6	5	4
0	1	2	3	4

What addends combine to put an 8 in the ones column?

2-digit sums

9
9

1-digit sums

9	8	7	6	5
0	1	2	3	4

What addends combine to put a 9 in the ones column?

33

MATHNIQUE ™
Money
You are
doing great!

NAME

MATHNIQUE ™
Money
You are
doing great!

NAME

MATHNIQUE ™
Money
You are
doing great!

NAME

MATHNIQUE ™
Money
You are
doing great!

NAME

MATHNIQUE ™
Money
You are
doing great!

NAME

MATHNIQUE ™
Money
You are
doing great!

NAME

MATHNIQUE ™
Money
You are
doing great!

NAME

MATHNIQUE ™
Money
You are
doing great!

NAME

MATHNIQUE ™
Money
You are
doing great!

NAME

MATHNIQUE ™
Money
You are
doing great!

NAME

SECTION III

LESSON PLANS AND SUPPORT MATERIAL

SECTION III   LESSON PLANS AND SUPPORT MATERIAL

© Learning Wrap-ups Inc. 1997

PREPROGRAM COUNTING and PRACTICE WITH MONEY

- Use the PreProgram PENNY PAGE with 20 numbered circles, p. 41.

- Each student needs 20 pennies for counting purposes. Have students put pennies on the circles and count the numbers aloud as they place the pennies on the chart in order. Repeat as needed.

- Have students remove the pennies starting at 20 and count backwards as pennies are removed. Repeat as needed.

- Give each student a dime. Explain that anytime they get to 10, they can trade 10 pennies for a dime.

- Explain that pennies are often called cents. 10 pennies are the same as 10 cents. 1 dime equals 10 pennies, or can be called 10 cents.

- Have students place 10 pennies on the circles. Have them change the 10 pennies for a dime. Place it on the 10 in the 10's column (dime column) add 3 pennies on the next row. How many cents do they have?

- Practice with various amounts. Examples: 5 pennies plus 4 pennies. Can you replace them with a dime? *No, there are not enough pennies.* 8 pennies plus 5 pennies. Can you put a dime on? *Yes!* How many pennies are left when you exchange 10 of them for a dime? *3.* How many cents do you have? *13¢.*

- Continue this line of thinking until students feel comfortable with the pennies, and with replacing 10 pennies with a dime.

- Extended activity: All of the above exercises can be used to do the inverse operation of subtraction. It is a good idea to help the students work both functions. Once they understand the relationship between add and subtract, all facts are easier to learn.

- Have students place a dime and 2 pennies on their chart. Ask what they would do if they had to give you 7 pennies. Help them understand that they need to change their dime to 10 pennies first. Then they can give you 7 pennies. Repeat the activities until students understand that dimes can be changed to pennies, and pennies can be changed to dimes whenever they need to be, so they can do a math problem. Tell students this is called regrouping.

- Write problems on the board so students can see what addition and subtraction problems look like.

- It is important that students be able to count forward and backward to 100. Use whatever materials are available to accomplish this task. Continually work on it. However, once students can count to 20, you can start with the 10 Secrets program.

- This book includes a "100 Circles All Purpose Counting Chart," p. 20. Use it to count forward and backward to 100. It can also be used to write to 100, to learn that 10 pennies equal a dime, and 10 dimes equal a dollar. Help students understand that it would take a penny on every circle on the chart to equal a dollar.

• Use real pennies with the students!

How do you get your pennies and dimes back? Keep each child's money in a paper cup. Pass out the paper cups. When it is time to collect, have students put their pennies on the circles and the dime in the center. As TEACHER checks, student puts money in cup and hands it back to the TEACHER.

LESSONS for the 1, 10, 100 FACTS

It is important to know that every addition/subtraction concept taught in this program, except regrouping, is taught with the 1, 2 and 3 facts. The purpose is to have students learn the **concept** with an easy fact, allowing all the mental effort to be centered only on the concept.

Students should be able to count to at least 20 forward and backward before starting this program.

1. **Use the 100 Circles All Purpose Counting Chart** to count pennies or other manipulatives, p.20. First add pennies, counting forward on the circles chart, then remove pennies, counting backward. Follow the directions for adding and subtracting with pennies on the circles chart. Teach counting to 100 forward and backward as soon as possible.

2. Add 1 Addition Facts   PENNY PAGE, p. 41. Have students use pennies on the circles chart to solve the problems. When the problems are finished, ask if there is anything they have noticed about the problems. Help them discover that when you are adding two numbers, it does not matter in which order the numbers come, the sum will always be the same as long as the same two numbers are used. Have them say the words "Commutative Property." Webster defines the words this way: *of or pertaining to an operation in which the order of the elements does not affect the result, as, in addition, 3 + 2 = 2 + 3 and, in multiplication, 2 X 3 = 3 X 2."*

3. Use the # 1 Addition LEARNING WRAP-UP
   - Teach students how to use the Learning Wrap-up. Be certain they hold it at the top. It is more difficult for younger children to hold the Wrap-up at the top, but insist they do so. It will pay off later as the children become faster and faster with the Wrap-ups.
   - Remind students to wrap the string from the top to the bottom. Always put the string up through the notch at the bottom when they have found the answers for all the problems. Show them how it keeps the string in place.
   - Talk to students about the lines on the back of the board. As they finish wrapping, they should check to make certain they have done it correctly. Tell them that the lines on the back of the board are for the students to see if there are any errors. If they can see a raised line, it can be corrected by unwinding and trying again. Remind students that Wrap-ups help them learn quickly and that you will know whether they are using them properly when you give the written test. Take the time necessary to learn how to use the Wrap-ups now. It will cut down the time it takes to learn new facts, as students become proficient with the Wrap-ups. In the beginning, insist they say the problems and answers aloud. This helps put the information in long term memory.

4. Listen to and sing with the audio cassette Addition WRAP-UP RAP #1. There are several ways teachers use this tape: 1. Number a paper in the same order as the problems on the Learning Wrap-up; have students write the answers before they are given on the tape. 2. Have students dance and sing with the tape, calling out the answers before they are given on the tape. 3. Have students wrap the Learning Wrap-up as the tape is played. (First and second grade students should have a great deal of practice with the Wrap-up before putting the audio tape and Wrap-up together.)

5. Subtract 1 Subtraction Facts PENNY PAGE, p. 42 Use pennies to work through the problems on this page. Ask students if they notice anything unusual about the answers to the problems.   Help them discover the relationship between the answer of one problem to the factor in the problem directly below it.   We will call these problems "Subtraction Buddies" and will be doing more work with them later on.

6. Follow with the #1 Subtraction LEARNING WRAP-UP and Subtraction WRAP-UP RAP.
    (See instructions 3 and 4.)

7. Talk about Vertical and Horizontal Problems, p. 43.

    Help students understand that both add and subtract problems can be written in different
    ways. We will use the two ways shown on this worksheet. Have students say each of the
    problems on the page aloud. Check to see if they understand by having them write 2
    vertical problems and 2 horizontal problems at the bottom of the page.

8. COMMUTATIVE PARTNERS and SUBTRACTION BUDDIES worksheets, p. 44.
    • Point out the relationship of the four problems across the top row. Do all of the problems
      across the row. If students need to use pennies to help them understand the concept, let them
      get the pennies out. When all 12 sets of problems are completed, students can cut the
      problems apart, scramble them then put the four related problems together with a paper clip.
    • If there is time, have students pair up and play the "Memory" game, using only the addition
      COMMUTATIVE PARTNERS, or only the SUBTRACTION BUDDIES.
    • Save problem slips in envelopes. They can be used as flash cards for practice if students
      leaves their Wrap-ups at home.

9. Add, Subtract 1 FACT FAMILY worksheet, p. 45.
    • This worksheet makes it very clear how the add and subtract families go together. It asks
      students to write the problems they were introduced to with along with the COMMUTATIVE
      PARTNERS and SUBTRACTION BUDDIES. Talk about 1+1=2, and why the problem next to
      it is exactly the same. What about 2-1? Point out that whenever we add the same numbers,
      we call them doubles. Who can think of other numbers to add that are doubles? 3 + 3, 5 +5,
      and so on.
    • There is no need to do doubles problems at this time. Have students work all the
      problems on the worksheet. Use the chalkboard or overhead as much as is necessary for
      all students to understand the concept. Then walk about the classroom checking to make
      certain each student understands.

10. Add 1 WORD PROBLEMS, p. 46.
    Read these problems aloud. Work them on the chalkboard as the students do them on
    their worksheets. These problems can easily be set up so students can make up some
    problems of their own. Whenever students have input, you will find them excited to
    create and produce. Have them suggest more problems that you can work on the
    chalkboard. Get out the Dollar, Dime and Penny Chart to solve the new problems they
    come up with.

11. Practice with the +1 and -1 LEARNING WRAP-UPS.
    Do each of the Wrap-ups for at least five minutes. This will prepare them to do the next page
    quickly.

12. Use the DOLLAR, DIME AND PENNY CHART (DDP), p. 21.
    • Show students what they know. Color and cut the substitute money if needed.
    • Make an overhead transparency or draw the DDP chart on the chalkboard. Have students
      put pennies on the chart: 2 pennies plus 1 penny equals 3 pennies, etc.
    • Explain that they can do the same problems with dimes. Have them work the exact same
      problems in the 10's column with the dimes. Show them that we write 10's or dimes with
      2 digits, using a 0 on the right side of our number to tell everyone we are talking about
      dimes (10's) and not pennies (1's). Explain that if we think about the penny (1) facts we
      know, we can use them to solve problems about dimes (10's). Show four or five 10's
      problems on the chalkboard or overhead.

13. Make an overhead transparency of **"If I know that..."** p. 47, or draw the boxes on the chalkboard.
   - Show students several examples of what they know. Show that if they can add numbers in the 1's column, they can add those same numbers in the 10's column and the 100's column as well.   Students should have no trouble with this concept.

14. Add, Subtract 10's FACT FAMILY, p. 48.
   - Reiterate the things you taught with the DDP chart and let students use it to work through the 10's problems on this page. Use the substitute dimes. Have students 1) color, 2) crumple the page; 3) press paper flat, then 4) cut dimes sections into small squares showing a dime in each square. Wrinkling the paper makes the substitute coins easier to pick up when students are working with them.
   - When students are comfortable with this concept, go immediately to the 100 Fact Family Format. *Show copious amounts of surprise and delight at how quickly students pick up this concept. Students love to please their teacher. Make certain they ALWAYS know they are doing it.*

15. Add, Subtract 100's FACT FAMILY, p. 49.
   - Review the things you taught with the DDP chart and let students use it to work through the problems on this page. Make certain they understand how much 100 is. If necessary, get the 100 Circles Chart, p. 20 out and explain that there would have to be a penny on every circle to have 100. Ask how many sheets of circles you would need for 500. What about 1200? For now, call it "twelve hundred." Ask if they would like to carry around all the pennies that would go on 9 sheets of paper. If you have several rolls of pennies, let students lift them to see how heavy they are. Explain that we are glad someone invented a system that we could write hundreds easily by putting the number followed by two zeros. Follow this line of thinking until students understand.
   - Have students complete the 100 FACT FAMILY WORKSHEET.

16. Use the overhead transparency **"If I know that... ,"** to put numbers other than 0 in each of the columns. Look ahead to the POWER PAGE, p. 50, to guide what you will be showing the students in this lesson. Work several problems so they will have confidence that they can do the next assignment. Explain how many problems they can do just by knowing 1 fact. Ask how many they think they could do if they knew 100 facts. (Any answer will do, but encourage them to say the biggest numbers they know.)

17. Complete the POWER PAGE, p. 50.

   - Discuss addition and subtraction of zero. Do several examples on the chalkboard, making certain every student understands, before assigning this page.
   - Have students work the problems from left to right. They will get extremely excited about how fast they can do the assignment and exude confidence upon completing the worksheet. It will also speed up their skills.   We will teach them later when it is better to work from right to left.
   - Be sure to let students know how incredible they are. Tell them you knew they could do this assignment fast, but you are astounded at how fast they worked.

18. Use the THINKER SHEET, p. 51.
   - Make certain the students thoroughly understand the 1 facts. Have 2 students work together to do the THINKER SHEET. One student reads the problems, the other gives the answers.
   - Then they trade, each student having the opportunity to give the answers by memory. Again, fold the paper in half if there are too many problems. They can complete the page in two or three sessions.

19. Add, Subtract 10, FACT FAMILY, p. 52.

   - Make certain students understand adding any number to "0" and subtracting "0" from any number. The SUBTRACTION BUDDIES can be treated as facts. When students are ready to color in the HERE'S WHAT I'VE LEARNED, p. 18, for the 1's, they will want to be able to fill in the 10's also.

   - Practice with the +10 and - 10 Learning Wrap-ups.

   Show students how to lay all 4 of the LEARNING WRAP-UP boards (+1, -1, +10, -10) on their desk with the strings hanging down. Then do all four of the Wrap-ups without stopping. Explain that we call this activity a WRAP-UP WRAP-OFF, and that before we know it, we will be able to have a WRAP-OFF with all of the boards. This practice will help them get ready.

   > What about 11? Treat it as one of the sets of facts. At this point students should be able to add and subtract 11. If they need more practice, use the REGROUPING SHEET, p 28, to create some extra problems for them. Point out that if they can add and subtract 1's and 10's they can add and subtract 11's. They will get more practice with "11" in each of the lessons. Don't be concerned about regrouping for now. Be sure to include the 11 facts when coloring the HERE'S WHAT I'VE LEARNED, p. 18.

20. Send home the +1, -1, +10, -10 LEARNING WRAP-UPS. Suggest they try a WRAP-OFF with their parents.

THE NEXT DAY

1. Give Quick Quiz for + - 1. Determine how fast your students need to write the answers to one column of the Quick Quiz. Allow that amount of time for students to write the answers. You may choose as long as a minute for younger children, and as little as 15 seconds for older students. Allow extra time for the subtraction column.

2. Have students color MATHNIQUE COLORING CHART (HERE'S WHAT I'VE LEARNED), p. 18. Follow the instructions on p. 8.

   > You may want to have one of these charts enlarged and laminated so that it can be used for the whole class year after year.

   SUGGESTIONS:

   - Have the students count aloud with you as you count the problems that have been colored in.

   - Invite the principal to come to your class and count with you.

   - Have the students write a note to their parents telling them how many facts they learned in just _____ days.

PREPROGRAM PENNY CHART

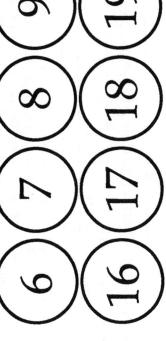

| 1 | 2 | 3 | 4 | 5 | 6 | 7 | 8 | 9 | 10 |
| 11 | 12 | 13 | 14 | 15 | 16 | 17 | 18 | 19 | 20 |

+ 1 PENNY PAGE   Use pennies to solve these problems.

1 + 1 = ☐☐ (shaded)

1 + 1 = ☐☐

2 + 1 = ☐☐   3 + 1 = ☐☐   4 + 1 = ☐☐   5 + 1 = ☐☐   6 + 1 = ☐☐

1 + 2 = ☐☐   1 + 3 = ☐☐   1 + 4 = ☐☐   1 + 5 = ☐☐   1 + 6 = ☐☐

7 + 1 = ☐☐   8 + 1 = ☐☐   9 + 1 = ☐☐   10 + 1 = ☐☐   11 + 1 = ☐☐   12 + 1 = ☐☐

1 + 7 = ☐☐   1 + 8 = ☐☐   1 + 9 = ☐☐   1 + 10 = ☐☐   1 + 11 = ☐☐   1 + 12 = ☐☐

Commutative Partners

Do the #1 Addition Learning Wrap-up and mark a square each time you do it correctly.

☒ ☐☐☐☐☐

The numbers in an addition problem can trade places and the answer is still the same. This is called commutative property. The numbers in these "add 1" problems help students understand. Use the penny chart above to show the concept.

Each student should have 20 pennies and the #1 Subtraction Learning Wrap-up.

1	2	3	4	5	6	7	8	9	**10**
11	12	13	14	15	16	17	18	19	**20**

-1 PENNY PAGE   Use pennies to solve these problems.

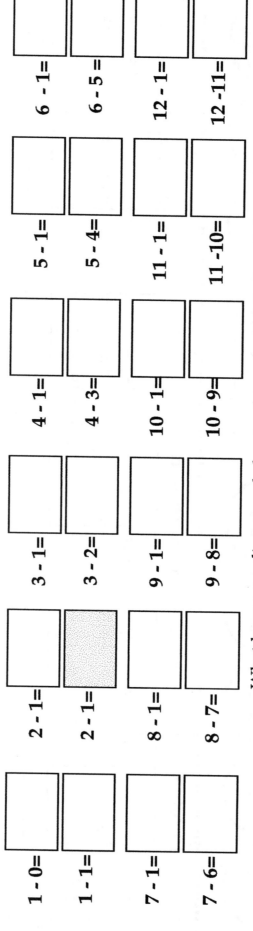

1 - 0 = ☐
1 - 1 = ☐

2 - 1 = ☐
2 - 1 = ☐

3 - 1 = ☐
3 - 2 = ☐

4 - 1 = ☐
4 - 3 = ☐

5 - 1 = ☐
5 - 4 = ☐

6 - 1 = ☐
6 - 5 = ☐

7 - 1 = ☐
7 - 6 = ☐

8 - 1 = ☐
8 - 7 = ☐

9 - 1 = ☐
9 - 8 = ☐

10 - 1 = ☐
10 - 9 = ☐

11 - 1 = ☐
11 -10 = ☐

12 - 1 = ☐
12 -11 = ☐

What have you discovered about subtraction while doing these problems?

Do the #1 Subtraction Learning Wrap-up and mark a square each time you do it correctly.

☒ ☐ ☐ ☐ ☐ ☐ ☐

Subtraction Buddies

Help students understand the inverse operation of subtraction. Explain that you can only "take away" when there is a big enough number to take away from. Pennies, crayons, books, students, counting cubes, plastic discs will work well as examples. Show the relationship between the two problems that are grouped together on this worksheet. For future references we will call them "Subtraction Buddies" in this program. Give examples with several real items. Continue to use pennies after the point has been clearly understood.

42

Here are two ways we can write add and subtract problems.
Problems that look like they are standing up are called vertical problems.

Sometimes they are in boxes so we can learn to write in a smaller space.

Sometimes the problems are not in a box, but the answers are still the same.

$$\begin{array}{r} 1 \\ +5 \\ \hline \end{array} \quad \begin{array}{r} 5 \\ +1 \\ \hline \end{array} \quad \begin{array}{r} 6 \\ -1 \\ \hline \end{array} \quad \begin{array}{r} 6 \\ -5 \\ \hline \end{array}$$

$$\begin{array}{r} 1 \\ +5 \\ \hline \end{array} \quad \begin{array}{r} 5 \\ +1 \\ \hline \end{array} \quad \begin{array}{r} 6 \\ -1 \\ \hline \end{array} \quad \begin{array}{r} 6 \\ -5 \\ \hline \end{array}$$

Sometimes problems look like they are laying down on the job.
We call them horizontal problems.

Sometimes they are in a box.   Sometimes they are not in a box.

The answers are still the same!

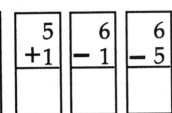

$1+5=$ ____ $5+1=$ ____

$6-1=$ ____ $6-5=$ ____

$1+5=$ ____ $5+1=$ ____

$6-1=$ ____ $6-5=$ ____

vertical	horizontal
$\begin{array}{r} 1 \\ +4 \\ \hline \end{array}$ or	$1+4=$ ____

vertical	horizontal
$\begin{array}{r} 4 \\ +1 \\ \hline \end{array}$ or	$4+1=$ ____

vertical	horizontal
$\begin{array}{r} 5 \\ -1 \\ \hline \end{array}$ or	$5-1=$ ____

vertical	horizontal
$\begin{array}{r} 5 \\ -4 \\ \hline \end{array}$ or	$5-4=$ ____

The answers are still the same!

Write 2 vertical problems.   Write 2 horizontal problems.

COMMUTATIVE PARTNERS

$1+1=$ _____	$1+1=$ _____
$2+1=$ _____	$1+2=$ _____
$3+1=$ _____	$1+3=$ _____
$4+1=$ _____	$1+4=$ _____
$5+1=$ _____	$1+5=$ _____
$6+1=$ _____	$1+6=$ _____
$7+1=$ _____	$1+7=$ _____
$8+1=$ _____	$1+8=$ _____
$9+1=$ _____	$1+9=$ _____
$10+1=$ _____	$1+10=$ _____
$11+1=$ _____	$1+11=$ _____
$12+1=$ _____	$1+12=$ _____

SUBTRACTION BUDDIES

$2-1=$ _____	$2-1=$ _____
$3-1=$ _____	$3-2=$ _____
$4-1=$ _____	$4-3=$ _____
$5-1=$ _____	$5-4=$ _____
$6-1=$ _____	$6-5=$ _____
$7-1=$ _____	$7-6=$ _____
$8-1=$ _____	$8-7=$ _____
$9-1=$ _____	$9-8=$ _____
$10-1=$ _____	$10-9=$ _____
$11-1=$ _____	$11-10=$ _____
$12-1=$ _____	$12-11=$ _____
$13-1=$ _____	$13-12=$ _____

1 FACT FAMILY

Use what you know to find the answer for each printed problem, then write all the problems that belong to the same family.

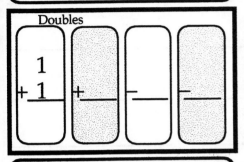

Doubles

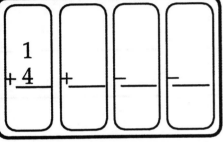

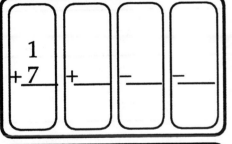

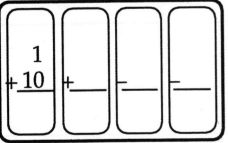

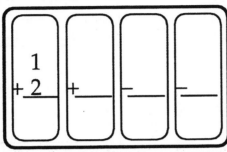

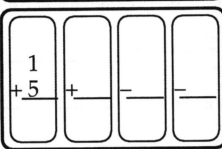

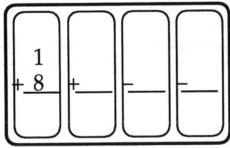

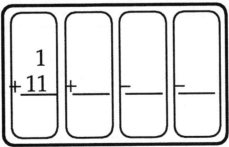

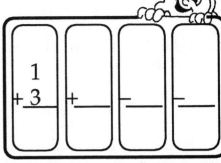

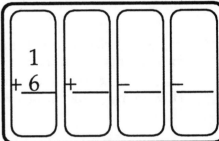

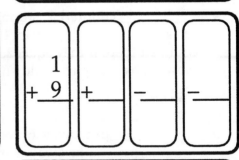

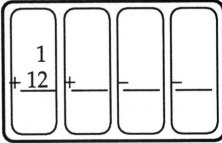

review

$1 + 5 =$ _____	$8 + 1 =$ _____	$8 - 1 =$ _____	$8 - 7 =$ _____
$1 + 10 =$ _____	$9 + 1 =$ _____	$10 - 1 =$ _____	$11 - 10 =$ _____
$1 + 8 =$ _____	$7 + 1 =$ _____	$12 - 1 =$ _____	$10 - 9 =$ _____
$1 + 9 =$ _____	$10 + 1 =$ _____	$9 - 1 =$ _____	$12 - 11 =$ _____
$1 + 11 =$ _____	$11 + 1 =$ _____	$11 - 1 =$ _____	$9 - 8 =$ _____
$1 + 6 =$ _____	$1 + 1 =$ _____	$13 - 1 =$ _____	$7 - 6 =$ _____

DOING MATH IN THE LUNCH ROOM.

All of the students in _____'s class went to the lunch room to do math problems. The students were to look for anything they could find to make up math problems. Here are some of the problems they wrote. Write the problem and answer, the commutative partner and the subtraction buddies.

1. _____counted 8 tables. _____found 1 more table behind the curtain. How many tables did they count?

addends and sum
$8 + 1 = 9$ tables

commutative partner
$1 + 8 = 9$ tables

subtraction buddies
$9 - 1 = 8$

$9 - 8 = 1$

2. _____ate 9 carrots. _____ate 1 carrot. How many carrots were eaten?

3. _____rinsed out 5 milk cartons for students to put their crayons in. _____rinsed out 1 more. How many milk cartons were rinsed out.

4. _____counted 7 students sitting at a table. _____ said 1 more person could sit there if they squeezed together. How many students could sit at the table?

5. _____put away 6 chairs. _____ put away 1 more chair. How many chairs did they put away?

6. _____ put biscuits on 3 trays. _____put biscuits on 1 tray. How many trays of biscuits in all?

7. _____ did 10 math problems. _____ did 1 math problem. What was the total problems they did?

$\underline{\qquad 10 + 1 = \qquad\qquad}$

Answer all of the problems in the two boxes.

$1+1=$ _____

$9+1=$ _____

$6+1=$ _____

$1+8=$ _____

$1+2=$ _____

$\begin{array}{r} 7 \\ +1 \\ \hline \end{array}$ $\begin{array}{r} 4 \\ +1 \\ \hline \end{array}$ $\begin{array}{r} 10 \\ +1 \\ \hline \end{array}$

$\begin{array}{r} 1 \\ +3 \\ \hline \end{array}$ $\begin{array}{r} 5 \\ +1 \\ \hline \end{array}$

$\begin{array}{r} 11 \\ +1 \\ \hline \end{array}$

Use for teaching overhead transparency.

Choose a +1 fact with a single digit answer.

pennies, cents or ones

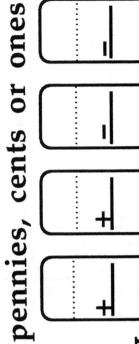

I know...

___ + ___ = ___

So... I know

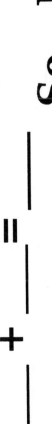

A. Use the same fact in both the 1's place and the 10's place.
B. Use the commutative partners and subtraction buddies in the 1's or 10's place.

dimes, 10 cents or tens

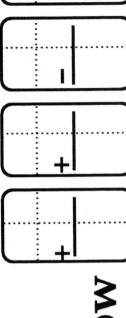

I know...

___ + ___ = ___

So...I know

___

A. Use the same fact in the 1's place, the 10's place and the 100's place.
B. Use the commutative partners or subtraction buddies and 0's in the 1' 10's or 100's place.

dollars, 100 cents or hundreds

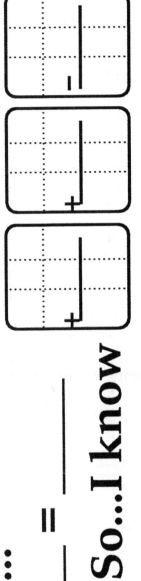

I also know...

___ + ___ = ___

So...I know

___

10's FACT FAMILY

Use what you know about "1's" (pennies) to find the answers for the "10's" (dimes). Then write all the problems that belong to the same family.

10
+ 00 | + ___ | ___ | ___

Doubles

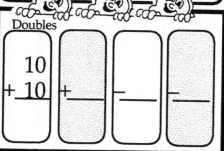

10
+ 10 | + ___ | ___ | ___

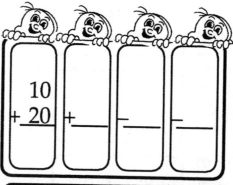

10
+ 20 | + ___ | ___ | ___

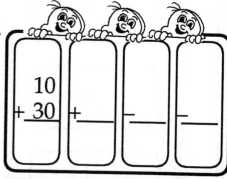

10
+ 30 | + ___ | ___ | ___

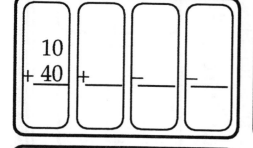

10
+ 40 | + ___ | ___ | ___

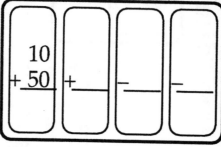

10
+ 50 | + ___ | ___ | ___

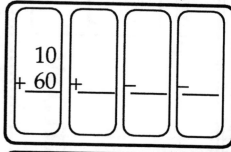

10
+ 60 | + ___ | ___ | ___

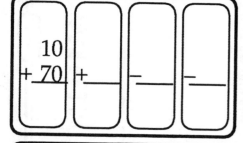

10
+ 70 | + ___ | ___ | ___

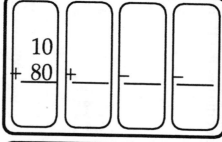

10
+ 80 | + ___ | ___ | ___

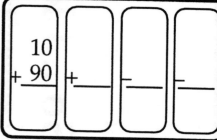

10
+ 90 | + ___ | ___ | ___

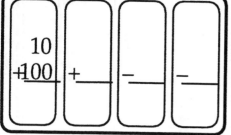

10
+100 | + ___ | ___ | ___

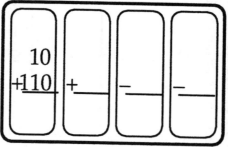

10
+110 | + ___ | ___ | ___

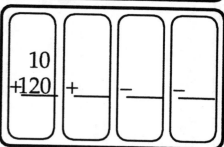

10
+120 | + ___ | ___ | ___

review

10 + 50 = ____	80 + 10 = ____	80 − 10 = ____	80 − 70 = ____
10 +100 = ____	90 + 10 = ____	100 − 10 = ____	110 −100 = ____
10 + 80 = ____	70 + 10 = ____	120 − 10 = ____	100 − 90 = ____
10 + 90 = ____	100 + 10 = ____	90 − 10 = ____	120 −110 = ____
10 +110 = ____	110 + 10 = ____	110 − 10 = ____	90 − 80 = ____
10 + 60 = ____	10 + 10 = ____	130 − 10 = ____	70 − 60 = ____

100 FACT FAMILY

"Can you do the 100's as fast as you can do the 1's?"

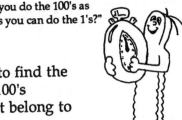

Use what you know about 1's (pennies) to find the answer for each printed problem about 100's (dollars), then write all the problems that belong to the same family of 100's (dollars).

$\begin{array}{r}100\\+000\end{array}$ $+\underline{\quad}$ $-\underline{\quad}$ $-\underline{\quad}$		

Doubles

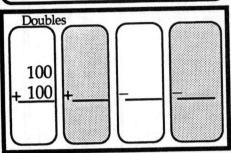

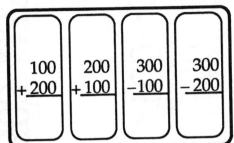

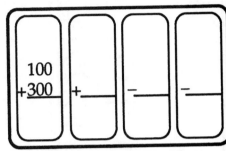

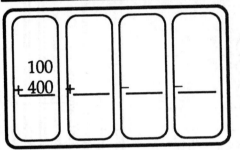

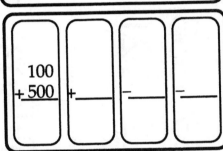

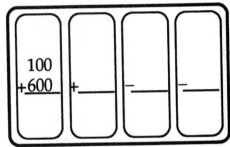

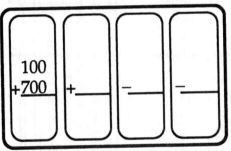

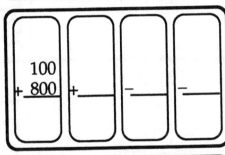

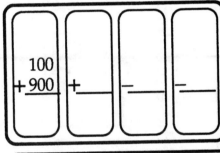

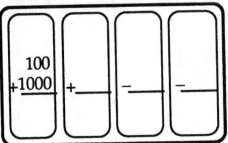

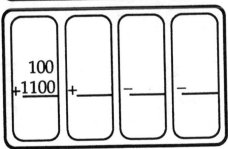

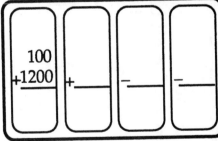

review

100 + 700 =_____	700 + 100 =_____	900 − 100 =_____	900 − 800 =_____
100 + 600 =_____	600 + 100 =_____	800 − 100 =_____	800 − 700 =_____
100 + 800 =_____	800 + 100 =_____	1000 − 100 =_____	1000 − 900 =_____
100 + 900 =_____	900 + 100 =_____	1100 − 100 =_____	1100 − 1000 =_____
100 + 300 =_____	300 + 100 =_____	500 − 100 =_____	500 − 400 =_____
100 + 500 =_____	500 + 100 =_____	700 − 100 =_____	700 − 600 =_____

POWER PAGE

I know that 2 + 1 = 3. So...
I can write the answers for all of these problems.

$$\begin{array}{r}1\\+2\\\hline\end{array}\qquad\begin{array}{r}10\\+20\\\hline\end{array}\qquad\begin{array}{r}11\\+22\\\hline\end{array}\qquad\begin{array}{r}20\\+10\\\hline\end{array}\qquad\begin{array}{r}21\\+12\\\hline\end{array}\qquad\begin{array}{r}22\\+11\\\hline\end{array}\qquad\begin{array}{r}100\\+200\\\hline\end{array}\qquad\begin{array}{r}111\\+222\\\hline\end{array}\qquad\begin{array}{r}101\\+202\\\hline\end{array}$$

Watch the signs!

$$\begin{array}{r}3\\-2\\\hline\end{array}\qquad\begin{array}{r}30\\-20\\\hline\end{array}\qquad\begin{array}{r}33\\-22\\\hline\end{array}\qquad\begin{array}{r}30\\-10\\\hline\end{array}\qquad\begin{array}{r}33\\-11\\\hline\end{array}\qquad\begin{array}{r}33\\-12\\\hline\end{array}\qquad\begin{array}{r}333\\-121\\\hline\end{array}\qquad\begin{array}{r}300\\-100\\\hline\end{array}\qquad\begin{array}{r}300\\-200\\\hline\end{array}$$

Watch the signs!

$$\begin{array}{r}222\\+111\\\hline\end{array}\qquad\begin{array}{r}102\\+201\\\hline\end{array}\qquad\begin{array}{r}201\\+102\\\hline\end{array}\qquad\begin{array}{r}121\\+212\\\hline\end{array}\qquad\begin{array}{r}330\\-210\\\hline\end{array}\qquad\begin{array}{r}303\\-202\\\hline\end{array}\qquad\begin{array}{r}303\\-101\\\hline\end{array}\qquad\begin{array}{r}333\\-222\\\hline\end{array}\qquad\begin{array}{r}333\\-212\\\hline\end{array}$$

A. Students work these problems from left to right, and say the answers aloud as they write.
B. Have students practice listening as you read some of the numbers. Tell them to think what the number looks like. They then write the number down.
C. This page can be used later as a THINKER SHEET for Mental Math. Two students work together. One says the problem, ie, "two hundred and twenty-two plus one hundred and eleven," the other student mentally computes and gives the answer.

50

> Two students work together. One reads the problems, the other gives the answers from memory. Take turns reading the problems.

Watch the signs!

+ - 1 THINKER SHEET

A.

| $\begin{array}{r}1\\ +1\\ \hline 2\end{array}$ | $\begin{array}{r}3\\ -2\\ \hline 1\end{array}$ | $\begin{array}{r}4\\ -3\\ \hline 1\end{array}$ | $\begin{array}{r}5\\ +1\\ \hline 6\end{array}$ | $\begin{array}{r}10\\ -1\\ \hline 9\end{array}$ | $\begin{array}{r}1\\ +4\\ \hline 5\end{array}$ | $\begin{array}{r}5\\ -1\\ \hline 4\end{array}$ |

B.

| $\begin{array}{r}1\\ +2\\ \hline 3\end{array}$ | $\begin{array}{r}11\\ +1\\ \hline 12\end{array}$ | $\begin{array}{r}1\\ -1\\ \hline 0\end{array}$ | $\begin{array}{r}12\\ +1\\ \hline 13\end{array}$ | $\begin{array}{r}11\\ -10\\ \hline 1\end{array}$ | $\begin{array}{r}8\\ +1\\ \hline 9\end{array}$ | $\begin{array}{r}1\\ +12\\ \hline 13\end{array}$ |

C.

| $\begin{array}{r}4\\ -1\\ \hline 3\end{array}$ | $\begin{array}{r}7\\ -6\\ \hline 1\end{array}$ | $\begin{array}{r}0\\ +1\\ \hline 1\end{array}$ | $\begin{array}{r}8\\ -7\\ \hline 1\end{array}$ | $\begin{array}{r}6\\ +1\\ \hline 7\end{array}$ | $\begin{array}{r}12\\ -11\\ \hline 1\end{array}$ | $\begin{array}{r}6\\ -1\\ \hline 5\end{array}$ |

D.

| $\begin{array}{r}1\\ +3\\ \hline 4\end{array}$ | $\begin{array}{r}9\\ +1\\ \hline 10\end{array}$ | $\begin{array}{r}10\\ -9\\ \hline 1\end{array}$ | $\begin{array}{r}7\\ +1\\ \hline 8\end{array}$ | $\begin{array}{r}1\\ +11\\ \hline 12\end{array}$ | $\begin{array}{r}2\\ +1\\ \hline 3\end{array}$ | $\begin{array}{r}6\\ -5\\ \hline 1\end{array}$ |

E.

| $\begin{array}{r}1\\ +5\\ \hline 6\end{array}$ | $\begin{array}{r}1\\ +9\\ \hline 10\end{array}$ | $\begin{array}{r}2\\ -1\\ \hline 1\end{array}$ | $\begin{array}{r}10\\ +1\\ \hline 11\end{array}$ | $\begin{array}{r}3\\ +1\\ \hline 4\end{array}$ | $\begin{array}{r}5\\ -4\\ \hline 1\end{array}$ | $\begin{array}{r}8\\ -1\\ \hline 7\end{array}$ |

F.

| $\begin{array}{r}9\\ -8\\ \hline 1\end{array}$ | $\begin{array}{r}1\\ +6\\ \hline 7\end{array}$ | $\begin{array}{r}9\\ -1\\ \hline 8\end{array}$ | $\begin{array}{r}1\\ -0\\ \hline 1\end{array}$ | $\begin{array}{r}11\\ -1\\ \hline 10\end{array}$ | $\begin{array}{r}1\\ +7\\ \hline 8\end{array}$ | $\begin{array}{r}1\\ +0\\ \hline 1\end{array}$ |

G.

| $\begin{array}{r}7\\ -1\\ \hline 6\end{array}$ | $\begin{array}{r}12\\ -1\\ \hline 11\end{array}$ | $\begin{array}{r}4\\ +1\\ \hline 5\end{array}$ | $\begin{array}{r}0\\ +1\\ \hline 1\end{array}$ | $\begin{array}{r}1\\ +10\\ \hline 11\end{array}$ | $\begin{array}{r}1\\ +8\\ \hline 9\end{array}$ | $\begin{array}{r}3\\ -1\\ \hline 2\end{array}$ |

H.

| $\begin{array}{r}10\\ +60\\ \hline 70\end{array}$ | $\begin{array}{r}50\\ +10\\ \hline 60\end{array}$ | $\begin{array}{r}60\\ -10\\ \hline 50\end{array}$ | $\begin{array}{r}80\\ -70\\ \hline 10\end{array}$ | $\begin{array}{r}40\\ -30\\ \hline 10\end{array}$ | $\begin{array}{r}30\\ +10\\ \hline 40\end{array}$ | $\begin{array}{r}90\\ -10\\ \hline 80\end{array}$ |

I.

| $\begin{array}{r}300\\ +100\\ \hline 400\end{array}$ | $\begin{array}{r}600\\ -500\\ \hline 100\end{array}$ | $\begin{array}{r}300\\ -100\\ \hline 200\end{array}$ | $\begin{array}{r}400\\ +100\\ \hline 500\end{array}$ | $\begin{array}{r}100\\ +200\\ \hline 300\end{array}$ | $\begin{array}{r}700\\ -600\\ \hline 100\end{array}$ | $\begin{array}{r}700\\ -100\\ \hline 600\end{array}$ |

"You're reaching higher! WOW!"

10 FACT FAMILY

Use what you know to find the answer for each printed problem, then write all the problems that go with them.

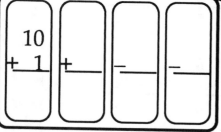

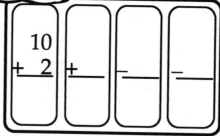

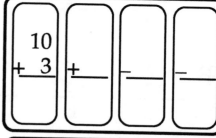

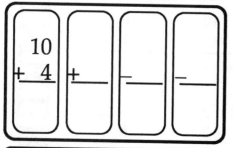

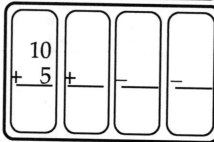

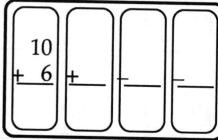

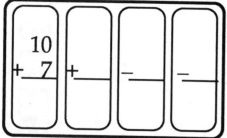

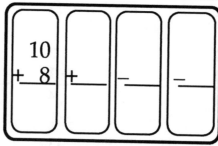

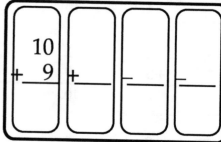

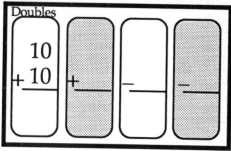

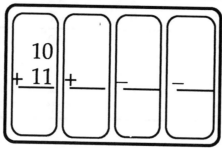

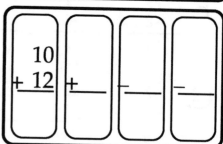

review

10 + 7 =_____	8 + 10 =_____	14 − 10 =_____	22 − 12 =_____
10 + 10 =_____	9 + 10 =_____	10 − 10 =_____	19 − 9 =_____
10 + 8 =_____	7 + 10 =_____	12 − 10 =_____	18 − 8 =_____
10 + 9 =_____	10 + 10 =_____	15 − 10 =_____	20 − 10 =_____
10 + 11 =_____	11 + 10 =_____	11 − 10 =_____	17 − 7 =_____
10 + 12 =_____	12 + 10 =_____	13 − 10 =_____	21 − 11 =_____

LESSON PLANS FOR TEACHING + - 2

> NOTE: Learning Wrap-ups for +2 and -2 should be sent home each day for as long as you are working with the #2 facts. The final Quick Quiz should be given first thing the day **after** the complete lesson has been taught and worksheets finished.

1. TALK ABOUT how easy it was to complete all of the work for 1's, 10's and 100's. Praise the students. Explain that now they know how to do all of the 1's problems, they will find that there is little difficulty doing the Add 2's, because they are going to use the same procedure as with 1's.

2. Do the +2 PENNY PAGE, p. 55. Be sure to use the pennies with the younger children. Students should use pennies to work through section A.

3. Pass out the **+2 Learning Wrap-up.** Have students practice wrapping it several times. Follow the instructions on the page. Write both horizontal and vertical problems on the chalkboard until you are certain the students understand what they are supposed to do. Do section B.

4. Wrap the +2 Learning Wrap-up and fill in the squares at the bottom of the page each time it is done correctly.

5. Take a break. Dance and say problems with the +2 Wrap-up Rap.

6. Do the - 2 PENNY PAGE, p. 56. Follow the same steps as in +2 PENNY PAGE.

   Practice on the **- 2 Learning Wrap-ups.** Try this method for the practice indicated under section B.

   > Write all of the problems and answers in the order they appear on the Wrap-up on the chalkboard. Say the problems and answers aloud. Students do the Wrap-up as they say it. Erase the 3 - 2 = 1 problem from the chalkboard. Say the problem aloud but do not say the answer. Finish the Wrap-up. Next erase 4 - 2 = 2. Go through the whole Wrap-up saying the problems aloud, leaving out the answers 1 and 2. Progress in this manner until the Wrap-up has been completed 12 times, each time leaving out one more answer.

   Be sure to mark a square each time you do the Wrap-up.

7. Do COMMUTATIVE PARTNERS and SUBTRACTION BUDDIES, p. 57. Have students look at the two sections (add and subtract). Show them how each of the four problems are related. Younger children can cut the problems apart, scramble them, then find the four related problems and put them in a group with a paper clip.

8. Use the Dollar, Dime and Penny Chart that is on p. 21, along with the add and subtract problems. Have students use their pennies and dimes as needed to complete this page of problems.

9. Do the "+ - 2 FACT FAMILY" worksheet, p. 59.

10. Do "+ 2 Word Problems" p. 60. Read them aloud. Have students write in the names of their classmates. Be sure they understand how to do each of the problems. Explain that they are simply writing the FACT FAMILY problems to go with each of the problems in the story.

11. Play the -2 Wrap-up Rap. Let students write the answers on paper before they are given on the tape, and call out the answers. Repeat as needed.

12. Do the 20 FACT FAMILY, p. 61.

13. Do the 200 FACT FAMILY, p, 62.

14. Do the POWER PAGE, p. 63. Explain how important every single fact is. Help students understand that each fact they know will give them the power to do hundreds of problems now, and millions of problems as they go through life.

15. Pair up to do the THINKER SHEET, p. 64.

16. Students should now have the power to do the + - 12 FACT FAMILY FORMAT, p. 65. Help them see what they know! Include the 12's when you do the Mathnique Coloring.

17. SEND HOME the +2 and -2 Learning Wrap-ups. Tell students to lay both Wrap-ups on the edge of the table with the strings hanging down, and to do both Wrap-ups as fast as they can.

THE NEXT DAY

- Have students do the + 2 and - 2 Learning Wrap-ups. Observe each student to be sure they practiced at home.

- Give the QUICK QUIZ for + - 2.

- FILL IN THE MATHNIQUE COLORING CHART (HERE'S WHAT I KNOW). Be sure to fill in the Commutative Partners and Subtraction Buddies! Repeat the process used after learning the 1's.

    Have the students count aloud with you as you count the problems that have been colored in.

    Invite the principal to come count with you.

    Have the students write a note to their parents telling them how many facts they learned in just _____ days.

    Count how many problems there are left to learn. Point out that in only two lessons they have learned almost half of all the facts they need to learn. PRAISE, PRAISE, PRAISE.

+2 PENNY PAGE Use pennies in the circles to complete these problems.

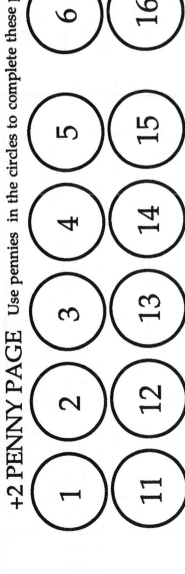

(1) (2) (3) (4) (5) (6) (7) (8) (9) (10)
(11) (12) (13) (14) (15) (16) (17) (18) (19) (20)

A. Use pennies to solve these ADDITION problems.

1 + 2 = ☐

2 + 2 = ☐

3 + 2 = ☐

4 + 2 = ☐

5 + 2 = ☐

6 + 2 = ☐

7 + 2 = ☐

8 + 2 = ☐

9 + 2 = ☐

10 + 2 = ☐

11 + 2 = ☐

12 + 2 = ☐

13 + 2 = ☐

14 + 2 = ☐

Each student should have 20 pennies. Have them find the answers to the problems in section A. Teach students to use the **#2 Addition Learning Wrap-up**, and do it 10 times while saying the problems and answers aloud. Tell students to correct their work by turning the Wrap-up over to see if the string covers the lines on the back.

Do the # 2 Addition Learning Wrap-up. Mark a square each time you do it correctly.

☒ ☐ ☐ ☐ ☐ ☐ ☐ ☐ ☐ ☐

What happens when we add 2?

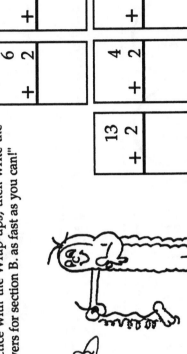

6 + 2	7 + 2	14 + 2
4 + 2	2 + 2	10 + 2
3 + 2	8 + 2	1 + 2

13 + 2   12 + 2

11 + 2

5 + 2

9 + 2

B. "Practice with the Wrap-ups, then write the answers for section B. as fast as you can!"

-2 PENNY PAGE

Always "take away" or subtract from the last pennies you put down.

| 1 | 2 | 3 | 4 | 5 | 6 | 7 | 8 | 9 | (10) |
| 11 | 12 | 13 | 14 | 15 | 16 | 17 | 18 | 19 | (20) |

A. Use pennies to solve these SUBTRACT (take-away) problems.

2 - 2 = ☐
3 - 2 = ☐
4 - 2 = ☐
5 - 2 = ☐
6 - 2 = ☐

7 - 2 = ☐
8 - 2 = ☐
9 - 2 = ☐
10 - 2 = ☐

11 - 2 = ☐
12 - 2 = ☐
13 - 2 = ☐
14 - 2 = ☐
15 - 2 = ☐

Do the #2 Subtract Learning Wrap-up. Mark a square each time you do it correctly.

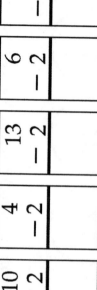

| ☐ | ☐ | ☐ | ☐ | ☐ |
| ☒ | ☐ | ☐ | ☐ | ☐ |

B. What happens when we subtract 2?

| 2
− 2 | 10
− 2 | 4
− 2 | 13
− 2 | 6
− 2 | 7
− 2 | 14
− 2 |
| 9
− 2 | 5
− 2 | 11
− 2 | 12
− 2 | 3
− 2 | 8
− 2 | 15
− 2 |

Each student should have 20 pennies. Use them to solve the problems in section A. **Teach students to use the #2 Subtraction Learning Wrap-up,** and do it at least 10 times while saying the problems and answers aloud. Tell them to correct their work by turning the Wrap-up over to see if the string covers the lines on the back.

COMMUTATIVE PARTNERS — SUBTRACTION BUDDIES

$1+2=\rule{1cm}{0.4pt}$	$2+1=\rule{1cm}{0.4pt}$	$3-2=\rule{1cm}{0.4pt}$	$3-1=\rule{1cm}{0.4pt}$
$2+2=\rule{1cm}{0.4pt}$	$2+2=\rule{1cm}{0.4pt}$	$4-2=\rule{1cm}{0.4pt}$	$4-2=\rule{1cm}{0.4pt}$
$3+2=\rule{1cm}{0.4pt}$	$2+3=\rule{1cm}{0.4pt}$	$5-2=\rule{1cm}{0.4pt}$	$5-3=\rule{1cm}{0.4pt}$
$4+2=\rule{1cm}{0.4pt}$	$2+4=\rule{1cm}{0.4pt}$	$6-2=\rule{1cm}{0.4pt}$	$6-4=\rule{1cm}{0.4pt}$
$5+2=\rule{1cm}{0.4pt}$	$2+5=\rule{1cm}{0.4pt}$	$7-2=\rule{1cm}{0.4pt}$	$7-5=\rule{1cm}{0.4pt}$
$6+2=\rule{1cm}{0.4pt}$	$2+6=\rule{1cm}{0.4pt}$	$8-2=\rule{1cm}{0.4pt}$	$8-6=\rule{1cm}{0.4pt}$
$7+2=\rule{1cm}{0.4pt}$	$2+7=\rule{1cm}{0.4pt}$	$9-2=\rule{1cm}{0.4pt}$	$9-7=\rule{1cm}{0.4pt}$
$8+2=\rule{1cm}{0.4pt}$	$2+8=\rule{1cm}{0.4pt}$	$10-2=\rule{1cm}{0.4pt}$	$10-8=\rule{1cm}{0.4pt}$
$9+2=\rule{1cm}{0.4pt}$	$2+9=\rule{1cm}{0.4pt}$	$11-2=\rule{1cm}{0.4pt}$	$11-9=\rule{1cm}{0.4pt}$
$10+2=\rule{1cm}{0.4pt}$	$2+10=\rule{1cm}{0.4pt}$	$12-2=\rule{1cm}{0.4pt}$	$12-10=\rule{1cm}{0.4pt}$
$11+2=\rule{1cm}{0.4pt}$	$2+11=\rule{1cm}{0.4pt}$	$13-2=\rule{1cm}{0.4pt}$	$13-11=\rule{1cm}{0.4pt}$
$12+2=\rule{1cm}{0.4pt}$	$2+12=\rule{1cm}{0.4pt}$	$14-2=\rule{1cm}{0.4pt}$	$14-12=\rule{1cm}{0.4pt}$

(TENS)   (ONES)

Take pennies off and put
a dime in the 10's column

Left	Dimes	Pennies	Subtraction	Addition
2 + 0 =	100	10	5 - 2 =	2 + __ = 5
2 + 6 =	90	9	11 - 2 =	6 + __ = 8
2 + 9 =	80	8	7 - 2 =	0 + __ = 2
2 + 3 =	70	7	3 - 2 =	2 + __ = 4
2 + 8 =	60	6	4 - 2 =	2 + __ = 9
2 + 5 =	50	5	2 - 2 =	8 + __ = 10
2 + 2 =	40	4	6 - 2 =	2 + __ = 7
2 + 7 =	30	3	9 - 2 =	10 + __ = 12
2 + 1 =	20	2	13 - 2 =	1 + __ = 3
2 + 4 =	10	1	8 - 2 =	2 + __ = 14
2 + 10 =			14 - 2 =	4 + __ = 6
2 + 11 =			12 - 2 =	2 + __ = 13
2 + 12 =			10 - 2 =	2 + __ = 11

DIMES   PENNIES

When you have finished this page, practice with the #2 Subtraction Learning Wrap-up.

2 FACT FAMILY

Use what you know to find the answer for each printed problem, then write all the problems that belong to the same family.

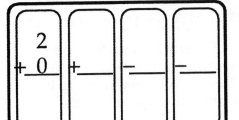

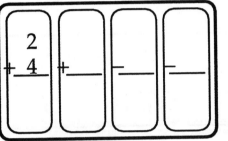

Doubles
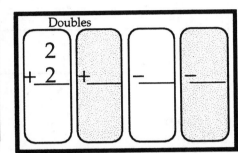

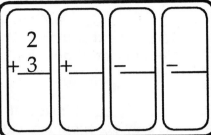

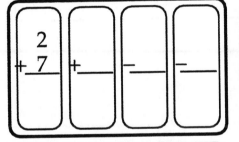

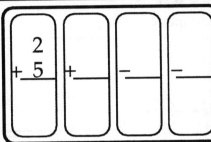

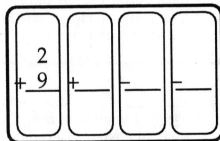

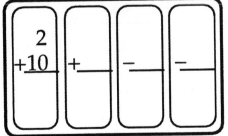

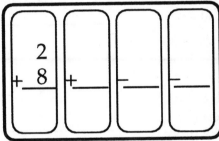

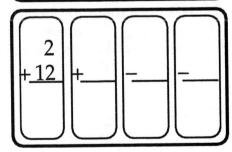

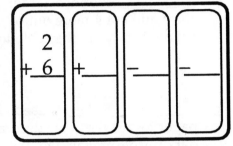

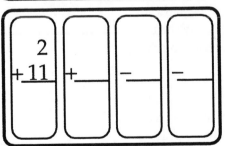

review

2 + 7 = _____	8 + 2 = _____	14 − 2 = _____	14 − 12 = _____
2 + 10 = _____	9 + 2 = _____	10 − 2 = _____	11 − 9 = _____
2 + 8 = _____	7 + 2 = _____	12 − 2 = _____	10 − 8 = _____
2 + 9 = _____	10 + 2 = _____	9 − 2 = _____	12 − 10 = _____
2 + 11 = _____	11 + 2 = _____	11 − 2 = _____	9 − 7 = _____
2 + 12 = _____	12 + 2 = _____	13 − 2 = _____	13 − 11 = _____

FISHING FOR MATH PROBLEMS

One day the students in our class cut fish out of colored paper, then we decorated them in different ways. Here are some word problems to tell about our project. We can write and solve the problems. We can also write the commutative partners and the subtraction buddies that use the same numbers.

1. _____ cut out 6 blue fish. _____ cut 2 more. What was the total number of blue fish?

2. _____'s piece of yellow paper was only big enough to cut out 2 fish. _____ found a larger piece that she could cut 4 more out of. How many yellow fish were they able to cut out?

3. _____ used lavender paper for his fish. He decorated 2 with dark purple crayon and 2 more with dark blue crayon. How many fish did he decorate with crayons?

4. _____ used several colors of paper to make 3 fish. Our teacher asked if anyone else could make more just like them. _____ and _____ made 2 more. What was the total of fish using several colors of paper?

5. It took _____ 9 minutes to decorate a green fish. Then it took only 2 minutes to decorate the next one. How many minutes did he spend on the fish project?

6. 2 students, _____ and _____ cut out 1 gold fish each. 8 other students cut out 1 silver fish each. What was the total of gold and silver fish they cut out?

20 FACT FAMILY

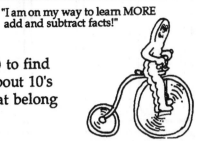

"I am on my way to learn MORE add and subtract facts!"

Use what you know about 1's (pennies) to find the answer for each printed problem about 10's (dimes), then write all the problems that belong to the same family of 10's (dimes).

20 +00	00 +20	20 −00	20 −20

20 +10	10 +20	30 −10	30 −20

Doubles

20 +20	+	−	−

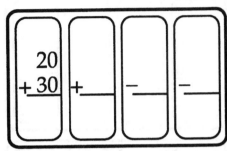

20 +30	+	−	−

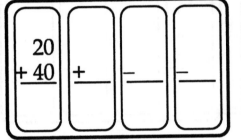

20 +40	+	−	−

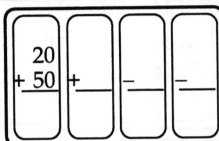

20 +50	+	−	−

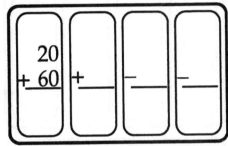

20 +60	+	−	−

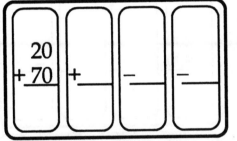

20 +70	+	−	−

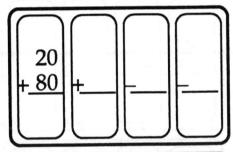

20 +80	+	−	−

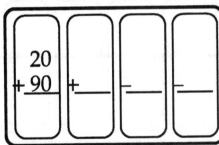

20 +90	+	−	−

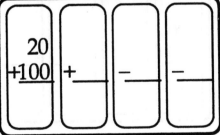

20 +100	+	−	−

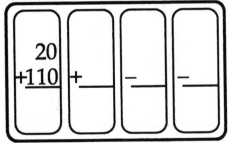

20 +110	+	−	−

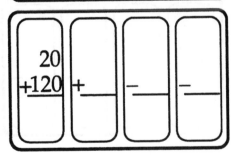

20 +120	+	−	−

review

20 + 70 = _____	70 + 20 = _____	90 − 20 = _____	90 − 70 = _____
20 + 60 = _____	60 + 20 = _____	80 − 20 = _____	80 − 60 = _____
20 + 80 = _____	80 + 20 = _____	100 − 20 = _____	100 − 80 = _____
20 + 90 = _____	90 + 20 = _____	110 − 20 = _____	110 − 90 = _____
20 + 30 = _____	30 + 20 = _____	50 − 20 = _____	50 − 30 = _____
20 + 50 = _____	50 + 20 = _____	70 − 20 = _____	70 − 50 = _____

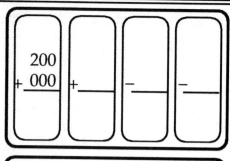

200 FACT FAMILY

"It doesn't take a Wizard to add hundreds when you know how to add ones."

Use what you know about 1's (pennies) to find the answer for each printed problem about 100's (dollars), then write all the problems that belong to the same family of 100's (dollars).

What do you notice about doing the doubles?

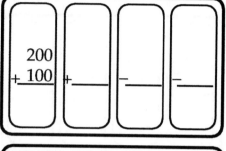

Doubles

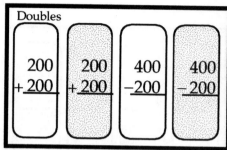

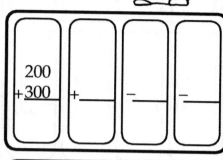

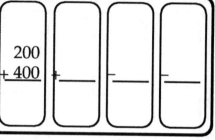

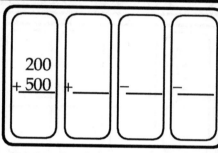

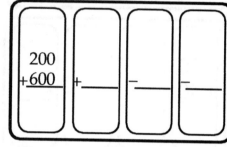

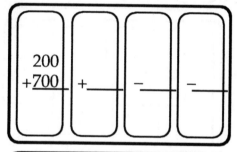

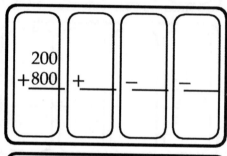

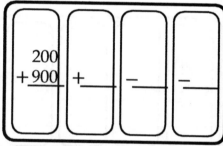

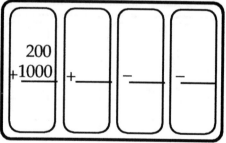

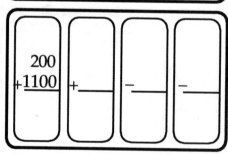

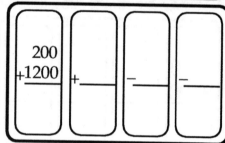

review

$200 + 700 =$ _____	$700 + 200 =$ _____	$900 - 200 =$ _____	$900 - 700 =$ _____
$200 + 600 =$ _____	$600 + 200 =$ _____	$800 - 200 =$ _____	$800 - 600 =$ _____
$200 + 800 =$ _____	$800 + 200 =$ _____	$1000 - 200 =$ _____	$1000 - 800 =$ _____
$200 + 900 =$ _____	$900 + 200 =$ _____	$1100 - 200 =$ _____	$1100 - 900 =$ _____
$200 + 300 =$ _____	$300 + 200 =$ _____	$500 - 200 =$ _____	$500 - 300 =$ _____
$200 + 500 =$ _____	$500 + 200 =$ _____	$700 - 200 =$ _____	$700 - 500 =$ _____

POWER PAGE

I know that 2 + 3 = 5.
Therefore, I know:

2 +3	3 +2	5 −3	5 −2

A.

2 +3	3 +2	20 +30	30 +20	22 +33	33 +22	23 +32	32 +23	200 +300	300 +200	220 +330	330 +220	202 +303

B.

303 +202	302 +203	203 +302	230 +320	320 +230	222 +333	333 +222	223 +332	332 +223	232 +323	323 +232	322 +233	233 +322

C.

5 −3	5 −2	50 −30	50 −20	55 −33	55 −22	55 −32	55 −23	500 −300	500 −200	550 −330	550 −220	505 −303

D.

505 −202	505 −302	505 −203	550 −230	550 −320	555 −222	555 −333	555 −332	555 −223	555 −323	555 −232	555 −233	555 −322

63

> Two students work together. One reads the problems, the other gives the answers from memory. Take turns reading the problems.

+ - 2 THINKER SHEET

Watch the signs!

A.

5	2	13	2	5	7	2
$+2$	$+2$	-2	$+5$	-3	-5	$+1$
3	4	11	7	2	2	3

B.

2	12	7	6	5	4	2
$+0$	-2	-2	$+2$	-2	$+2$	$+12$
2	10	5	8	3	6	14

C.

0	10	10	2	8	6	4
$+2$	-8	-2	-1	-2	-2	-2
2	2	8	1	6	4	2

D.

6	11	8	2	10	3	13
-4	-9	-6	$+8$	$+2$	-2	-11
2	2	2	10	12	1	2

E.

2	9	14	2	2	2	2
$+11$	-7	-2	$+4$	-2	-0	$+7$
13	2	12	6	0	2	9

F.

2	2	3	2	5	2	6	2
$+1$	$+9$	-2	$+3$	-2	$+5$	$+2$	$+7$
3	11	1	5	3	7	8	9

G.

20	40	50	10	80	90	12	60
$+20$	-20	-20	$+20$	$+20$	$+20$	-10	-40
40	20	30	30	100	110	2	20

H.

70	70	80	60	30	80	50	120
-20	-50	-60	-20	-10	-20	-30	-20
50	20	20	40	20	60	20	100

I.

400	200	120	700	600	500	400	200
$+200$	$+100$	-20	-200	$+200$	-200	$+200$	$+800$
600	300	100	500	800	300	600	1000

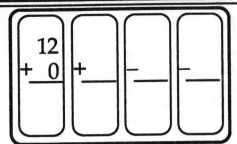

12 FACT FAMILY FORMAT

Use what you know to find the answer for each printed problem, then write all the problems that belong to the same family.

> Twelve is not considered one of the facts. It has been put in the fact family format here because it helps you understand that if you can add 2 and 10, you can add and subtract 12.

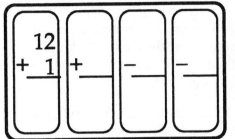

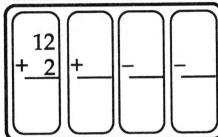

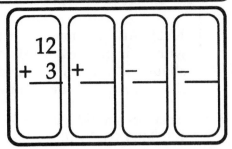

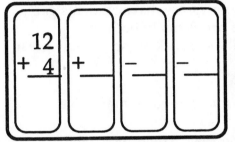

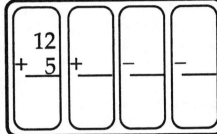

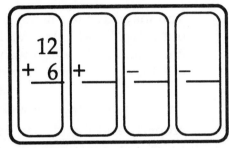

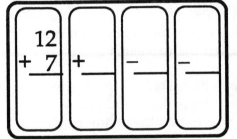

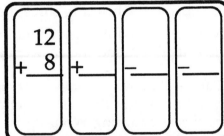

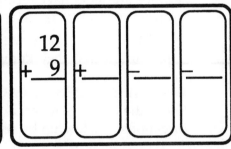

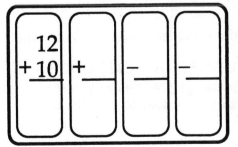

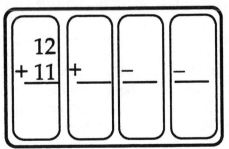

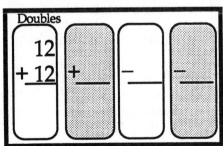

review

12 + 7 = _____	8 + 12 = _____	24 − 12 = _____	24 − 12 = _____
12 + 6 = _____	9 + 12 = _____	20 − 12 = _____	21 − 9 = _____
12 + 8 = _____	7 + 12 = _____	23 − 12 = _____	20 − 8 = _____
12 + 9 = _____	6 + 12 = _____	18 − 12 = _____	18 − 6 = _____
12 + 11 = _____	11 + 12 = _____	24 − 12 = _____	19 − 7 = _____
12 + 12 = _____	12 + 12 = _____	21 − 12 = _____	23 − 11 = _____

LESSON PLANS FOR TEACHING + - 3

> This and other lesson plans do not include a certain number of days in which they should be completed because of the wide range of skills students have when they start the program. To complete this program as quickly as possible, it is necessary to use Learning Wrap-ups in the classroom every day. Extra benefits are derived from them if they are used at least once in the morning and again in the afternoon. Then send the appropriate Wrap-ups home so parents will become involved with the program.

1. TALK ABOUT how much the students have accomplished. Tell them how pleased you are with their progress. Talk about learning the "3" facts. Ask them what they already know about 3's. Write all of the problems and answers on the chalkboard. Give students a blank sheet of paper so they can write down what they know.

   Answers should include 3+1, 1+3, 3+2, 2+3, 3+10, 10+3, 3+11, 11+3, 12+3, 3+12, 3-1, 3-2, 3-3, 4-3, 5-3, 13-3, 13-10, 14-3, 14-11, 15-3, 15-12. Also include 3+0, 0+3, and 3-0.

   You may have to remind them of what they have learned. If necessary, have students get out their "HERE'S WHAT I'VE LEARNED" Chart. Write the problems in both the horizontal and vertical forms so that they are all over the chalkboard. Rave about how great it is they could come up with all these problems and answers.

2. TALK ABOUT how easy it was to solve them all, when they understood commutative property and the inverse operation of subtraction.
   - Once students have all the problems and answers written on their papers, erase the answers and have students come to the board to solve the problems.
   - TELL students not to worry if they have forgotten about how much they know, but it is important that they know that they can find the answers when the problems come up.

3. Work with the PENNY PAGE for + 3, p. 69. As they start, have them look for problems they know the answers to, and write the answers first. Then get out the pennies and follow the directions. Follow up by using the **+3 Learning Wrap-up** as directed on the penny page.

4. Take a break. Dance and say problems with the +3 WRAP-UP RAP.

5. Work the PENNY PAGE for - 3, p. 70. Follow directions on the sheet for doing the Wrap-ups.

6. Write the answers to the COMMUTATIVE PARTNERS AND SUBTRACTION BUDDIES on p. 71. Cut into separate problems. Have students pair up and play a "memory" game, keeping any 2 related pairs. (Keep the strips in an envelope in their folder to practice with if they forget to return their Wrap-ups from home.)

7. Listen to and call out the answers for the - 3 WRAP-UP RAP.

8. Do the + - 3 FACT FAMILY worksheet, p. 72.

9. Do + 3 Word Problems, p. 73.

10. Do + - 30 FACT FAMILY worksheet, p. 74.

11. Have students cut and prepare (color, crinkle, spread smooth and cut out) the **dimes and dollars** on their SUBSTITUTE MONEY sheet, p. 28 if necessary. Use real dimes if possible.

12.   Get out the DOLLAR, DIME and PENNY CHART, p. 21. Each student should have a copy. Make a transparency of the chart to teach this lesson or draw it on the chalkboard.

13. **TALK ABOUT REGROUPING IN ADDITION**

Question students until you are certain they each understand ....

A penny is worth **1¢**.
A penny column could also be called the **ONE's** column or the **1's** column.

A dime is worth **10¢**.
A dime column could also be called the **TEN's** column or the **10's** column.

A dollar is worth **100¢**.
A dollar column could also be called the **HUNDRED's** column or the **100's** column.

Use the DOLLAR, DIME and PENNY CHART, p. 21, to do the following activities.

Have students place coins on the chart to show the following amounts.
Tell them not to take any coins off their paper until you tell them the next amount, then they can take off any extras.

7   37   137   248   196

- Have students remove all the coins.
- Tell them to put down 8 pennies. Add 3 pennies.
- Ask if they can trade any coins for a dime?
- What coins could be traded? (Trade 10 pennies for 1 dime.)
- Then we could say, when adding, 8 and 3 are a regrouping pair!
- Any time two 1 digit numbers add up to more than 10, they need to be regrouped.
- Explain that it is called "regrouping" whenever we can change 10 pennies for a dime or need to change a dime for 10 pennies.

Do several examples of trading pennies for a dime and a dime for 10 pennies.

Explain that whenever a 3 is part of the addition problem, there are only three number pairs that call for regrouping.   What are they?

$3 + 7 = 10$ $3 + 8 = 11$ $3 + 9 = 12$.

Point out that when we <u>first</u> start doing problems with <u>regrouping</u>, it is easier to work the problem from <u>right to left.</u> So we will do that as we work the next page.

Hand out + - 3 REGROUPING PAIRS worksheet, p. 75.
  (You may want to make an overhead transparency of p. 75 to do these problems with the students.) Work as many problems as necessary to be certain students can do them on their own.
Use the DOLLAR, DIME and PENNY Chart to work each of the problems.

  Ask students to put down the coins necessary to show 27. Add 3 coins. Do they need to change pennies for a dime?   Point out that the 7 and the 3 have been circled because they are a regrouping pair. They total 10 pennies. We change the 10 pennies for 1 dime. Now we have 0 pennies and 1 dime, so we write a 0 in the one's column answer space, and put a 1 at the top in the ten's column. Now we can add that dime to the other 2 dimes and the answer is 30, (3 dimes.)

Repeat the process with problem #2.
Put down coins to show 53. Add 9 pennies.
Do they need to change any pennies for a dime.
How many dimes do they have? Are there any pennies?
What is the answer to problem #2?

Have students circle the regrouping pair in problem #3. Can they do the problem without using their pennies and dimes?

Work through problems 3, 4, and 5.

Use the DOLLAR, DIME and PENNY Chart as long as is necessary.

TALK ABOUT REGROUPING WITH SUBTRACTION starting with problem #6.

Now we will be subtracting. Have students put down 2 dimes.
Ask if they can subtract 3 pennies.
Have them trade one of the dimes for 10 pennies.
Show them how to write a small 10 above the 0, and to write a 1 above the 2.
Cross out both the 2 and the 0.
Subtract the 3 from the small 10 in the 1's column $(10 - 3 = 7)$
Write 7 in the 1's column answer space.
Have students put their pencil on the small 1 in the 10's column. Ask if there is
    any number to subtract from the 1. $(1 - nothing = 1)$
Show them where to write the 1 in the answer space.

If more practice is necessary at this point, use the REGROUPING BLANK SHEET, p. 28 and dictate some problems for them to write down. If you are walking about the classroom checking students' work, you will know if they understand which numbers belong in which columns. Give extra help where needed.

Completing this page is a major accomplishment. Tell the students how proud you are of them. Tell them that this has been a gigantic step. Once they can do this kind of regrouping, they can do almost any of the worksheets in this book.

Have students give themselves a BIG CHEER!!!!!!

14. Do the 300 FACT FAMILY, p. 76.

15. Do the POWER PAGE for + - 3, p. 77. There are no regrouping pairs on this sheet. Tell students this is a reward for working so hard on the regrouping page. Because there is no regrouping, remind students to work the problems from left to right!!!

16. Pair up students to do the THINKER SHEET, p. 78. Tell them how important it is to say the answers quickly.

17. Send home the **+ 3 and - 3 Learning Wrap-ups.**

NEXT DAY

- Have students do the + 3 and - 3 Wrap-ups.

- Give the + - 3 QUICK QUIZ. Be sure to walk about the classroom as students are doing the quiz. It will help you determine if the class is ready to mark the "HERE'S WHAT I KNOW", Mathnique Coloring chart.

- Color the 3's on the "HERE'S WHAT I KNOW" chart.

+3 PENNY PAGE   Start putting the pennies down on 1.

(1) (2) (3) (4) (5) (6) (7) (8) (9) **(10)**

(11) (12) (13) (14) (15) (16) (17) (18) (19) **(20)**

Do the #3 Addition Learning Wrap-up.
Mark a square each time you do it correctly.

☒ ☐ ☐ ☐ ☐ ☐ ☐ ☐ ☐ ☐ ☐

A. Use pennies to solve these problems.

1 + 3 = ☐   6 + 3 = ☐   10 + 3 = ☐

2 + 3 = ☐   7 + 3 = ☐   11 + 3 = ☐

3 + 3 = ☐   8 + 3 = ☐   12 + 3 = ☐

4 + 3 = ☐   9 + 3 = ☐   13 + 3 = ☐

5 + 3 = ☐   14 + 3 = ☐

B. Use pennies to solve these problems if necessary.

1 + 3	2 + 3	3 + 3	4 + 3	5 + 3	6 + 3
7 + 3	8 + 3	9 + 3	10 + 3	11 + 3	12 + 3
3 + 1	3 + 4	3 + 10	3 + 7	3 + 8	3 + 5
3 + 12	3 + 2	3 + 3	3 + 6	3 + 9	3 +11

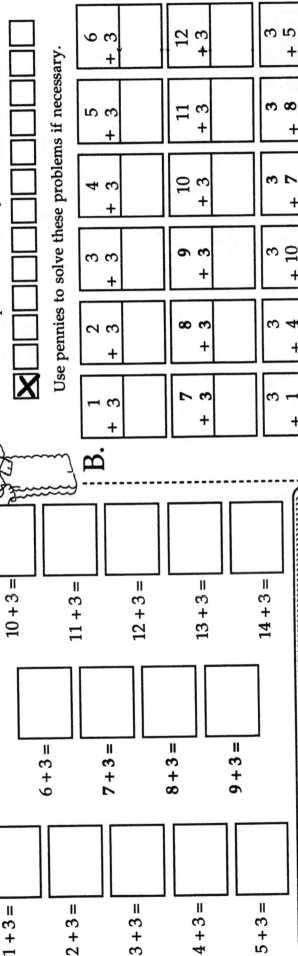

Each student should have 20 pennies. Be certain students get these 14 problems correct. If students are ready, make the exchange, 10 pennies for a dime. Give extra help with 7+3, 8+3, and 9+3.

Remind students of the commutative properties of addition, before they do the next set of problems. Let students keep this paper on their desk while doing Wrap-ups. Tell them not to look down at the answers unless they really need to. Practice with the #3 Addition Learning Wrap-up at least 10 times.

Do section B. Use pennies only if necessary.

-3 PENNY PAGE

Put pennies down starting with 1.   Subtract by taking away from the last penny you put down.

1	2	3	4	5	6	7	8	9	10
11	12	13	14	15	16	17	18	19	20

A.   Use pennies to solve these SUBTRACT problems.

$3 - 3 =$ ☐ $4 - 3 =$ ☐ $5 - 3 =$ ☐ $6 - 3 =$ ☐ $7 - 3 =$ ☐

$8 - 3 =$ ☐ $9 - 3 =$ ☐ $10 - 3 =$ ☐ $11 - 3 =$ ☐

$12 - 3 =$ ☐ $13 - 3 =$ ☐ $14 - 3 =$ ☐ $15 - 3 =$ ☐ $16 - 3 =$ ☐

Practice the #3 Subtraction Wrap-up.
Mark a square each time you do it correctly.

☒ ☐ ☐ ☐ ☐ ☐ ☐ ☐ ☐ ☐ ☐

B.   Use pennies to solve these problems if necessary.

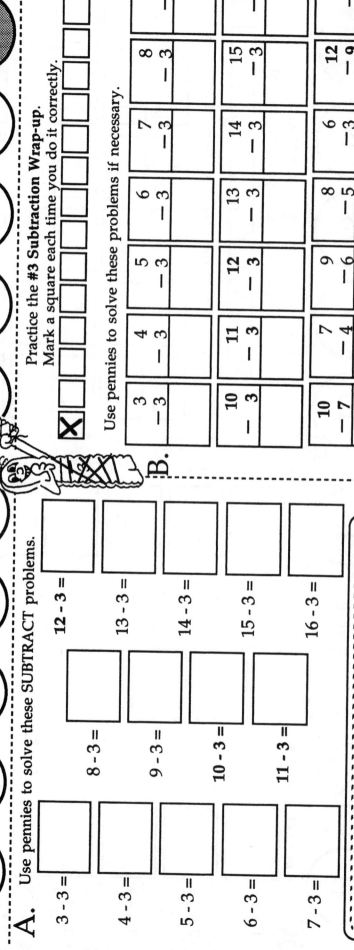

$3 \\ -3$	$4 \\ -3$	$5 \\ -3$	$6 \\ -3$	$7 \\ -3$	$8 \\ -3$	$9 \\ -3$
$10 \\ -3$	$11 \\ -3$	$12 \\ -3$	$13 \\ -3$	$14 \\ -3$	$15 \\ -3$	$16 \\ -3$
$10 \\ -7$	$7 \\ -4$	$9 \\ -6$	$8 \\ -5$	$6 \\ -3$	$12 \\ -9$	$11 \\ -8$
$14 \\ -11$	$13 \\ -10$	$3 \\ -0$	$12 \\ -9$		$4 \\ -1$	$5 \\ -2$

Each student should have 20 pennies and a dime.

Do section A.   Remind students that they always start laying down
the pennies on number 1.   When they (take away) SUBTRACT, they
start taking away from the last penny they put down.

Do the #3 Subtraction Learning Wrap-up 10 times. Have the students
say each problem and answer aloud as they do the Wrap-up.

Do section B. Think about "Subtraction Buddies."

COMMUTATIVE PARTNERS		SUBTRACTION BUDDIES	
$1+3=$ ___	$3+1=$ ___	$4-3=$ ___	$4-1=$ ___
$2+3=$ ___	$3+2=$ ___	$5-3=$ ___	$5-2=$ ___
$3+3=$ ___	$3+3=$ ___	$6-3=$ ___	$6-3=$ ___
$4+3=$ ___	$3+4=$ ___	$7-3=$ ___	$7-4=$ ___
$5+3=$ ___	$3+5=$ ___	$8-3=$ ___	$8-5=$ ___
$6+3=$ ___	$3+6=$ ___	$9-3=$ ___	$9-6=$ ___
$7+3=$ ___	$3+7=$ ___	$10-3=$ ___	$10-7=$ ___
$8+3=$ ___	$3+8=$ ___	$11-3=$ ___	$11-8=$ ___
$9+3=$ ___	$3+9=$ ___	$12-3=$ ___	$12-9=$ ___
$10+3=$ ___	$3+10=$ ___	$13-3=$ ___	$13-10=$ ___
$11+3=$ ___	$3+11=$ ___	$14-3=$ ___	$14-11=$ ___
$12+3=$ ___	$3+12=$ ___	$15-3=$ ___	$15-12=$ ___

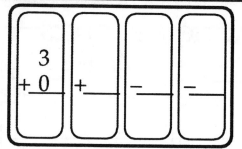

3 FACT FAMILY

"I'm flying right into the middle of the math facts."

Use what you know to find the answer for each printed problem, then write all the problems that belong to the same family.

The number pairs that will require regrouping have been circled. Which ones are they?

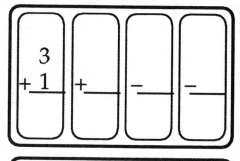

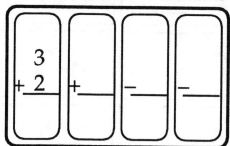

Doubles

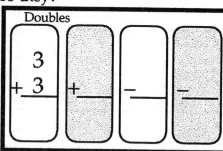

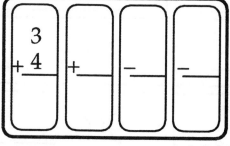

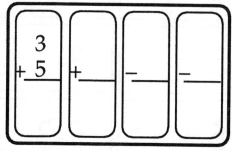

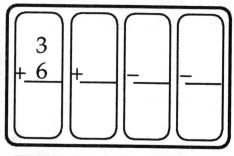

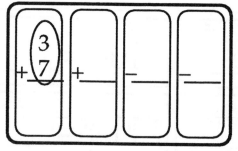

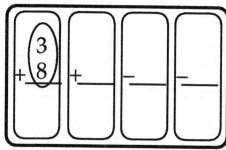

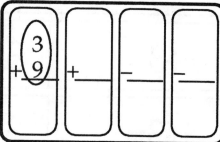

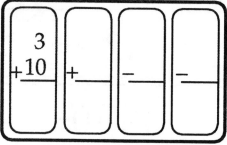

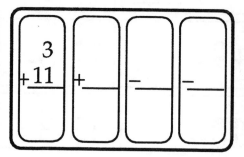

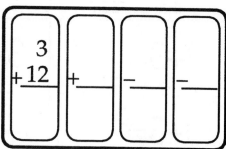

review

3 + 7 = _____	8 + 3 = _____	6 − 3 = _____	9 − 6 = _____
3 + 3 = _____	9 + 3 = _____	10 − 3 = _____	12 − 9 = _____
3 + 8 = _____	7 + 3 = _____	12 − 3 = _____	11 − 8 = _____
3 + 9 = _____	6 + 3 = _____	9 − 3 = _____	7 − 4 = _____
3 + 6 = _____	4 + 3 = _____	7 − 3 = _____	10 − 7 = _____
3 + 4 = _____	3 + 3 = _____	11 − 3 = _____	6 − 3 = _____

WARMING UP TO WORD PROBLEMS

It was a cold day and everyone wore gloves or mittens to school. We decided to practice some of our math problems with our gloves. We can write the problem, the commutative partner, and the subtraction buddies for each word problem!

1. _____ put 8 pairs of gloves in the center of a big circle. Then _____put in 3 pairs of mittens. How many pairs were there all together?

    $8 + 3 =$ _____ $11 - 8 =$ _____

    $3 + 8 =$ _____ $11 - 3 =$ _____

2. _____counted 3 pairs of green gloves. _____ counted 3 pairs of green mittens. How many green pairs in all?

    _____   _____

    _____   _____

3. _____ found 6 students with gloves that had matching hats. _____ found 3 more students who had the same color on their gloves, as was on their hats. How many students in these two groups?

    _____   _____

    _____   _____

4. _____ saw several pairs of gloves that had different colored fingers. Those students were asked to put on their gloves and hold up two fingers. _____ counted 7 white fingers and 3 red fingers. How many red and white fingers were held up?

    _____   _____

    _____   _____

5. After the math games were over, and the gloves were put back in their coat pockets, _____ thought of one more problem. He said there were 7 gloves hanging out of pockets, and 3 gloves had fallen on the floor. How many gloves needed to be stuffed deeper into the coat pockets?

    _____   _____

    _____   _____

6. 5 students said they liked to make up the word problems. 3 students said they liked it better when the teacher made them up. How many students expressed their opinion?

    _____   _____

    _____   _____

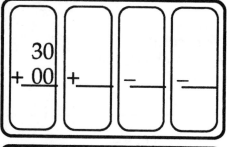

30 FACT FAMILY FORMAT

Use what you know to find the answer for each printed problem, then write all the problems that belong to the same family.

Circle the number pairs that will need to be regrouped.

"I love to work problems with regrouping!"

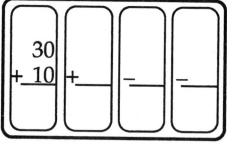 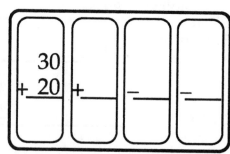 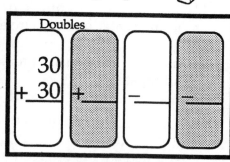

Doubles

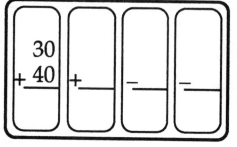 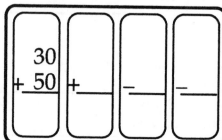 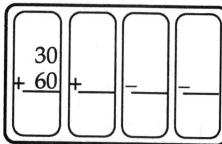

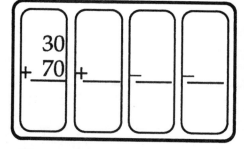 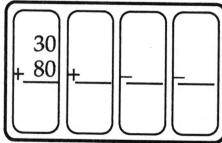 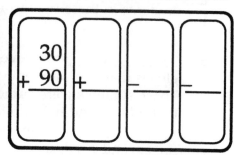

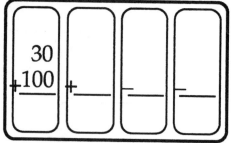 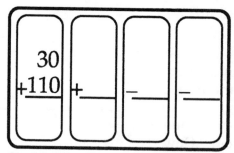 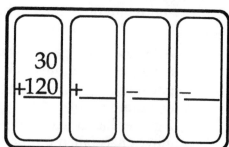

review

30 + 70 = _____	80 + 30 = _____	60 − 30 = _____	90 − 60 = _____
30 + 30 = _____	90 + 30 = _____	100 − 30 = _____	120 − 90 = _____
30 + 80 = _____	70 + 30 = _____	120 − 30 = _____	110 − 80 = _____
30 + 90 = _____	60 + 30 = _____	90 − 30 = _____	70 − 40 = _____
30 + 60 = _____	40 + 30 = _____	70 − 30 = _____	100 − 70 = _____
30 + 40 = _____	30 + 30 = _____	110 − 30 = _____	60 − 30 = _____

ADD Use the DOLLAR, DIME and PENNY CHART to work these problems.

"Now I get to do these fun problems!"

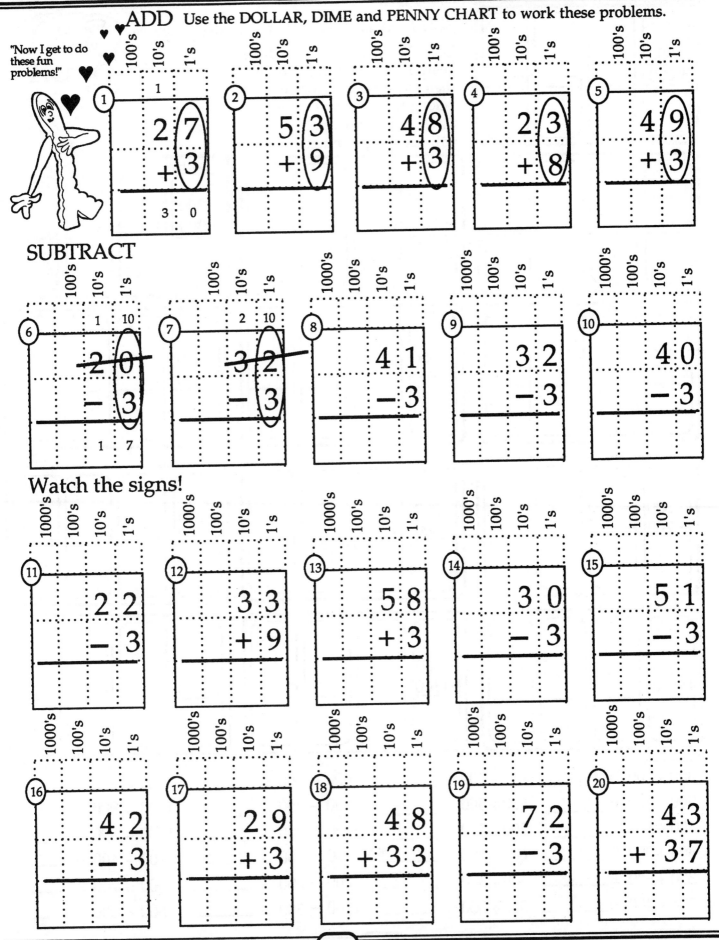

SUBTRACT

Watch the signs!

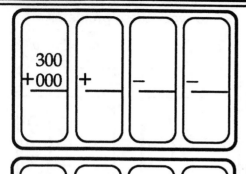

300 FACT FAMILY

Use what you know to find the answer for each printed problem, then write all the problems that belong to the same family.
Circle the number pairs that will need regrouping.

"Did you say the FAT family?"

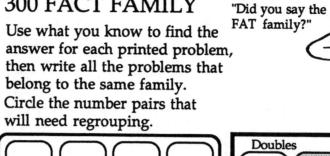

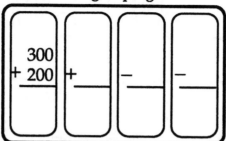

Doubles

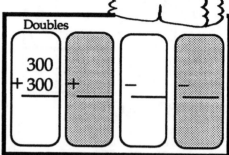

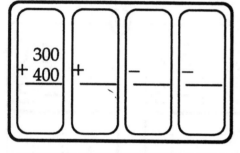

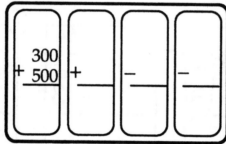

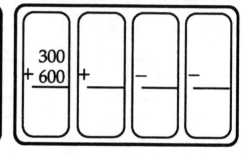

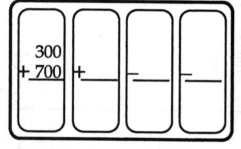

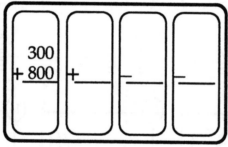

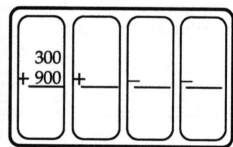

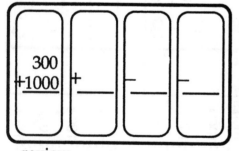

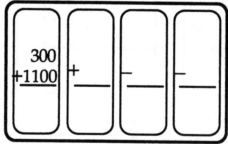

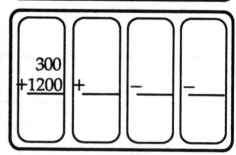

review

300 + 700 = _____	800 + 300 = _____	600 − 300 = _____	900 − 600 = _____
300 + 300 = _____	900 + 300 = _____	1000 − 300 = _____	1200 − 900 = _____
300 + 800 = _____	700 + 300 = _____	1200 − 300 = _____	1100 − 800 = _____
300 + 900 = _____	600 + 300 = _____	900 − 300 = _____	700 − 400 = _____
300 + 600 = _____	400 + 300 = _____	700 − 300 = _____	1000 − 700 = _____
300 + 400 = _____	300 + 300 = _____	1100 − 300 = _____	600 − 300 = _____

POWER PAGE

I know that 3 + 4 = 7
Therefore, I know...

and I can do all of
these problems!!!

3 + 4 ―― 7	4 + 3 ―― 7	7 - 3 ―― 4	7 - 4 ―― 3

3 + 4	30 + 40	40 + 30	33 + 44	44 + 33	34 + 43	43 + 34	300 + 400	400 + 300	330 + 440	440 + 330	303 + 404

| 404
+ 303 | 403
+ 304 | 304
+ 403 | 340
+ 430 | 430
+ 340 | 333
+ 444 | 444
+ 333 | 443
+ 334 | 334
+ 443 | 343
+ 434 | 434
+ 343 | 433
+ 344 | 344
+ 433 |

| 7
- 4 | 7
- 3 | 70
- 40 | 70
- 30 | 77
- 44 | 77
- 33 | 77
- 43 | 77
- 34 | 700
- 400 | 700
- 300 | 770
- 440 | 770
- 330 | 707
- 404 |

| 707
- 303 | 707
- 403 | 707
- 304 | 770
- 340 | 770
- 430 | 777
- 333 | 777
- 444 | 777
- 443 | 777
- 334 | 777
- 434 | 777
- 343 | 777
- 344 | 777
- 433 |

77

Two students work together. One reads the problems, the other gives the answers from memory. Take turns reading the problems.

Watch the signs!

A.

| $\begin{array}{r}3\\+4\\\hline 7\end{array}$ | $\begin{array}{r}8\\+3\\\hline 11\end{array}$ | $\begin{array}{r}6\\-3\\\hline 3\end{array}$ | $\begin{array}{r}3\\+6\\\hline 9\end{array}$ | $\begin{array}{r}12\\-3\\\hline 9\end{array}$ | $\begin{array}{r}10\\+3\\\hline 13\end{array}$ | $\begin{array}{r}7\\-3\\\hline 4\end{array}$ |

B.

| $\begin{array}{r}15\\-3\\\hline 12\end{array}$ | $\begin{array}{r}3\\+3\\\hline 6\end{array}$ | $\begin{array}{r}12\\-9\\\hline 3\end{array}$ | $\begin{array}{r}3\\-2\\\hline 1\end{array}$ | $\begin{array}{r}3\\+11\\\hline 14\end{array}$ | $\begin{array}{r}3\\+2\\\hline 5\end{array}$ | $\begin{array}{r}6\\-3\\\hline 3\end{array}$ |

C.

| $\begin{array}{r}0\\+3\\\hline 3\end{array}$ | $\begin{array}{r}8\\-5\\\hline 3\end{array}$ | $\begin{array}{r}11\\-3\\\hline 8\end{array}$ | $\begin{array}{r}6\\+3\\\hline 9\end{array}$ | $\begin{array}{r}5\\-2\\\hline 3\end{array}$ | $\begin{array}{r}9\\+3\\\hline 12\end{array}$ | $\begin{array}{r}7\\-4\\\hline 3\end{array}$ |

D.

| $\begin{array}{r}10\\-3\\\hline 7\end{array}$ | $\begin{array}{r}13\\-10\\\hline 3\end{array}$ | $\begin{array}{r}5\\+3\\\hline 8\end{array}$ | $\begin{array}{r}3\\-3\\\hline 0\end{array}$ | $\begin{array}{r}3\\+3\\\hline 6\end{array}$ | $\begin{array}{r}5\\-3\\\hline 2\end{array}$ | $\begin{array}{r}4\\-1\\\hline 3\end{array}$ |

E.

| $\begin{array}{r}3\\+0\\\hline 3\end{array}$ | $\begin{array}{r}3\\-0\\\hline 3\end{array}$ | $\begin{array}{r}10\\-7\\\hline 3\end{array}$ | $\begin{array}{r}8\\-3\\\hline 5\end{array}$ | $\begin{array}{r}7\\-3\\\hline 4\end{array}$ | $\begin{array}{r}3\\+9\\\hline 12\end{array}$ | $\begin{array}{r}3\\+10\\\hline 13\end{array}$ |

F.

| $\begin{array}{r}40\\-30\\\hline 10\end{array}$ | $\begin{array}{r}10\\+30\\\hline 40\end{array}$ | $\begin{array}{r}70\\+30\\\hline 100\end{array}$ | $\begin{array}{r}90\\-60\\\hline 30\end{array}$ | $\begin{array}{r}30\\+10\\\hline 40\end{array}$ | $\begin{array}{r}30\\-20\\\hline 10\end{array}$ | $\begin{array}{r}60\\-30\\\hline 30\end{array}$ | $\begin{array}{r}50\\+30\\\hline 80\end{array}$ |

G.

| $\begin{array}{r}30\\+10\\\hline 40\end{array}$ | $\begin{array}{r}20\\+30\\\hline 50\end{array}$ | $\begin{array}{r}50\\-30\\\hline 20\end{array}$ | $\begin{array}{r}70\\-40\\\hline 30\end{array}$ | $\begin{array}{r}60\\+30\\\hline 90\end{array}$ | $\begin{array}{r}30\\+70\\\hline 100\end{array}$ | $\begin{array}{r}90\\-30\\\hline 60\end{array}$ | $\begin{array}{r}30\\+90\\\hline 120\end{array}$ |

H.

| $\begin{array}{r}800\\+300\\\hline 1100\end{array}$ | $\begin{array}{r}400\\-300\\\hline 100\end{array}$ | $\begin{array}{r}300\\+500\\\hline 800\end{array}$ | $\begin{array}{r}400\\+300\\\hline 700\end{array}$ | $\begin{array}{r}600\\-300\\\hline 300\end{array}$ | $\begin{array}{r}800\\-300\\\hline 500\end{array}$ | $\begin{array}{r}500\\-300\\\hline 200\end{array}$ | $\begin{array}{r}900\\-600\\\hline 300\end{array}$ |

Say: eleven hundred.

I.

| $\begin{array}{r}500\\+300\\\hline 800\end{array}$ | $\begin{array}{r}200\\+100\\\hline 300\end{array}$ | $\begin{array}{r}900\\-600\\\hline 300\end{array}$ | $\begin{array}{r}400\\+300\\\hline 700\end{array}$ | $\begin{array}{r}700\\-400\\\hline 300\end{array}$ | $\begin{array}{r}900\\+300\\\hline 1200\end{array}$ | $\begin{array}{r}300\\+700\\\hline 1000\end{array}$ | $\begin{array}{r}600\\-300\\\hline 300\end{array}$ |

Say: twelve hundred

LESSON PLANS FOR TEACHING + - 4

> Students enjoy doing an activity called a **"Wrap-up Wrap-off."** Simply lay each of the Learning Wrap-ups they have studied on the edge of their desks with the strings hanging down. Then they wrap all of the boards as quickly as possible. With older students, it is a great challenge to complete all the boards in a certain amount of time. Younger children may be content with just completing them. Doing this activity once a day helps students to remember what they have learned up to this point.

1. Have students show they returned their Wrap-ups, but retain them at their desks.

2. Talk about how many + - 4 problems they have to learn.
   Point out that because of the commutative property, they already know 4+1, 1+4, 4+2, 2+4 4+3, 3+4, 5-4, 6-4, 7-4 11-4, 12-4. Remind students that they know 16-4, 15-4, 10+4, and 14-4 also. Praise!! Praise!!! Praise!!!!

3. Have a WRAP-OFF with the 2 and 3 Wrap-ups for review.

4. Work with + - 4 PENNY PAGES, pp. 80, 81. Do the + - Learning Wrap-ups as indicated on the worksheet.

5. Dance and say problems with the +4 WRAP-UP RAP.

6. Write the COMMUTATIVE PARTNERS and SUBTRACTION BUDDIES, p. 82.

7. Do the 4 FACT FAMILY worksheet, p. 83. Have students circle the regrouping pairs of numbers. Explain that being able to identify the numbers quickly will help them so they can do the problems faster and faster.

8. Do +4 WORD PROBLEMS, p. 84.

9. Practice the +4 and -4 Wrap-ups several times.

10. Do the 40 FACT FAMILY worksheet, p.85.

11. Do the + - 4 REGROUPING PAGE, p. 86. All of the regrouping pairs are in the 1's column. Do not tell the students, but have them identify the regrouping pairs by drawing a light circle around them. The subtract problems can be prepared by doing the regrouping first, then working the problems from left to right! Get out the DOLLAR, DIME and PENNY Chart to work through these problems.

12. Do 400 FACT FAMILY, p. 87.

13. Do 4 + 5 POWER PAGE, p. 88. Ask if there are any regrouping pairs. When they discover there are not, tell them to work the problems from left to right.

14. Pair up to do the 4 THINKER SHEET, p. 89.

15. Have a "WRAP-OFF" with the 1, 2, 3 Addition Wrap-ups, then have a second WRAP-OFF with the 1, 2, 3 Subtraction Wrap-ups. Allow more time for the subtraction.

16. SEND HOME the +4 and -4 Wrap-ups. Tell students to practice each Wrap-up at least 10 times. You will be having a "Wrap-off" with the + - 3 and + - 4 Wrap-ups tomorrow.

NEXT DAY

- Do + - 4 QUICK QUIZ and color in the "HERE'S WHAT I KNOW" Chart. Be sure to have students color in the charts in their folders as well.

USE PENNIES OR MARKERS IN THE CIRCLES TO COMPLETE THESE PROBLEMS

NAME _____

+4 PENNY PAGE   Always start at 1 when using the number circles to solve problems.

| 1 | 2 | 3 | 4 | 5 | 6 | 7 | 8 | 9 | 10 |
| 11 | 12 | 13 | 14 | 15 | 16 | 17 | 18 | 19 | 20 |

A. Use pennies or discs to solve these problems.

1 + 4 = ☐

2 + 4 = ☐

3 + 4 = ☐

4 + 4 = ☐

5 + 4 = ☐

6 + 4 = ☐

7 + 4 = ☐

8 + 4 = ☐

9 + 4 = ☐

10 + 4 = ☐

11 + 4 = ☐

12 + 4 = ☐

13 + 4 = ☐

14 + 4 = ☐

15 + 4 = ☐

Each student should have 20 pennies. When appropriate, replace 10 pennies with a dime.

Remind students of the commutative properties of addition, before they do the next set of problems.

Use the **#4 Addition Learning Wrap-up**, and do it several times. Be sure to say the problems and answers aloud.

Fold the paper before doing section B.

B.

Do the **#4 Addition Learning Wrap-up**. Mark a square each time you do it correctly.

☐☐☐☐☐☐☐☐☐☐☐☐☐☐☐

Use pennies to solve these problems if necessary.

1 + 4	2 + 4	3 + 4	4 + 4	5 + 4	6 + 4
7 + 4	8 + 4	9 + 4	10 + 4	11 + 4	12 + 4
4 + 1	4 + 4	4 + 10	4 + 7	4 + 8	4 + 5
4 + 12	4 + 2	4 + 3	4 + 6	4 + 9	4 + 11

© Learning Wrap-ups Inc. 1997

- 4 PENNY PAGE

Use pennies on the circles to solve the problems.

NAME _____   # _____

Always start at 1 when covering the number circles to solve problems. To take-away or subtract, start removing pennies from the last circle you covered.

Number circles:

1	2	3	4	5	6	7	8	9	10
11	12	13	14	15	16	17	18	19	20

(10 and 20 are shaded)

A. Use pennies or discs to solve these problems.

$4 - 4 =$ ☐	$14 - 4 =$ ☐
$5 - 4 =$ ☐	$15 - 4 =$ ☐
$6 - 4 =$ ☐	$16 - 4 =$ ☐
$7 - 4 =$ ☐	$17 - 4 =$ ☐
$8 - 4 =$ ☐	$18 - 4 =$ ☐
$9 - 4 =$ ☐	
$10 - 4 =$ ☐	
$11 - 4 =$ ☐	
$12 - 4 =$ ☐	
$13 - 4 =$ ☐	

Do the #4 Subtraction Learning Wrap-up. Mark a square each time you do it correctly.

☒ ☐ ☐ ☐ ☐ ☐ ☐ ☐ ☐ ☐

B. Use pennies to solve these problems if necessary.

$4 - 4$	$5 - 4$	$6 - 4$	$7 - 4$	$8 - 4$	$9 - 4$
$10 - 4$	$11 - 4$	$12 - 4$	$13 - 4$	$14 - 4$	$15 - 4$
$6 - 4$	$10 - 4$	$4 - 4$	$8 - 4$	$11 - 4$	$9 - 4$
$5 - 4$	$14 - 4$	$15 - 4$	$13 - 4$	$7 - 4$	$12 - 4$

Each student should have 20 pennies and 1 dime. Be certain students have all the answers in section A correct. Trade 10 pennies for a dime when appropriate.

Use the #4 Subtraction Learning Wrap-up, and do it at least 10 times. Be sure to say the problems and answers aloud.

Fold paper in half, and do section B for practice.

COMMUTATIVE PARTNERS | SUBTRACTION BUDDIES

1+4=___	4+1=___	5-4=___	5-1=___
2+4=___	4+2=___	6-4=___	6-2=___
3+4=___	4+3=___	7-4=___	7-3=___
4+4=___	4+4=___	8-4=___	8-4=___
5+4=___	4+5=___	9-4=___	9-5=___
6+4=___	4+6=___	10-4=___	10-6=___
7+4=___	4+7=___	11-4=___	11-7=___
8+4=___	4+8=___	12-4=___	12-8=___
9+4=___	4+9=___	13-4=___	13-9=___
10+4=___	4+10=___	14-4=___	14-10=___
11+4=___	4+11=___	15-4=___	15-11=___
12+4=___	4+12=___	16-4=___	16-12=___

4 FACT FAMILY

Use what you know to find the answer for each printed problem, then write all the problems that belong to the same family.

"Look how quickly you can do these problems. They're a cinch!"

Circle the pairs that total 10 or more.

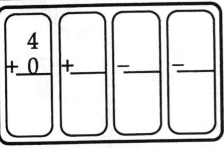

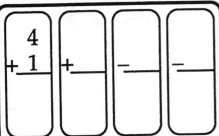

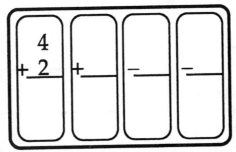

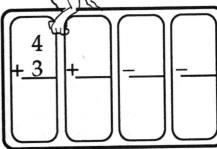

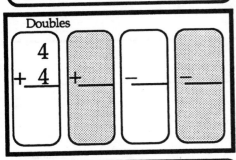

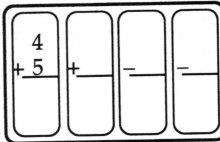

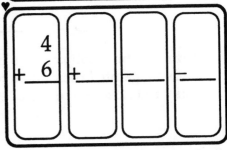

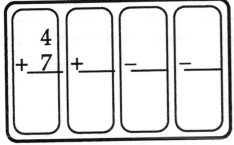

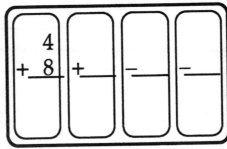

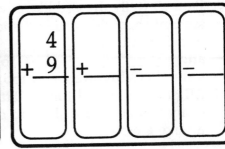

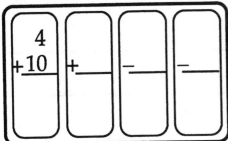

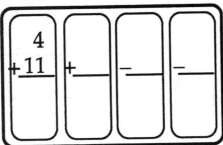

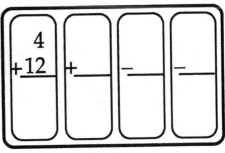

review

4 + 7 = _____	8 + 4 = _____	14 − 4 = _____	16 − 12 = _____
4 + 10 = _____	9 + 4 = _____	10 − 4 = _____	13 − 9 = _____
4 + 8 = _____	7 + 4 = _____	12 − 4 = _____	12 − 8 = _____
4 + 9 = _____	10 + 4 = _____	9 − 4 = _____	14 − 10 = _____
4 + 11 = _____	11 + 4 = _____	11 − 4 = _____	11 − 7 = _____
4 + 12 = _____	12 + 4 = _____	13 − 4 = _____	15 − 11 = _____

CLOWNING AROUND WITH ADD 4

Our teacher _____read a book about Emmett Kelly, a famous circus clown. We liked it so much our teacher decided that we could have a clown day at school. Look at all the problems we can do using the 4 FACTS! Solve the problem then write the commutative partner and subtraction buddies that belong to the problem in the story.

1. 4 students, _____
_____, _____
and _____ wore
frizzy orange hair. 5 other students
had rainbow colored frizzy hair. How
many students had frizzy hair?

_____   _____

_____   _____

2. _____, _____,
_____ and _____ all
had red rubber ball noses. 6 other
students painted their noses red. How
many red noses were there?

_____   _____

_____   _____

3. Emmett Kelly dressed like a hobo. 4
students had old worn-out shoes.
But 2 students, _____,
and_____, found
some shoes that were way too big.
All of them looked funny. How
many students used shoes to dress
up like a clown?

_____   _____

_____   _____

4. 8 students painted their faces with
brown coloring to look like beards.
4 others painted their faces with black
coloring. How many painted their
faces?

_____   _____

_____   _____

5. The principal, _____, came into
our class wearing a pair of pants with big
baggy pockets. One pocket had 9 pieces of
caramel candy. Another pocket had 4
pieces of butterscotch. How many pieces
of candy were in those two pockets?

_____   _____

_____   _____

40 FACT FAMILY

Use what you know to find the
answer for each printed problem,
then write all the problems that
belong to the same family.

"TRY THIS!"

"Write the sums for the
families that have an odd
number in the 10's column
first. Then solve the rest
of the problems as fast as
you can."

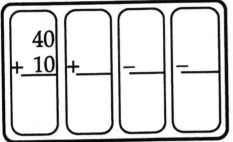

$$\begin{array}{r} 40 \\ +\ 0 \\ \hline \end{array}$$

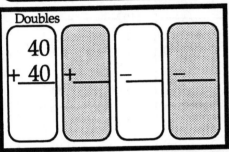

$$\begin{array}{r} 40 \\ +\ 10 \\ \hline \end{array}$$

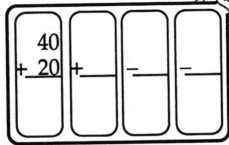

$$\begin{array}{r} 40 \\ +\ 20 \\ \hline \end{array}$$

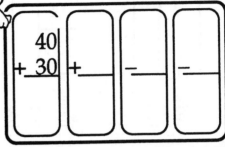

$$\begin{array}{r} 40 \\ +\ 30 \\ \hline \end{array}$$

Doubles

$$\begin{array}{r} 40 \\ +\ 40 \\ \hline \end{array}$$

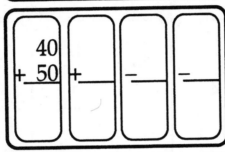

$$\begin{array}{r} 40 \\ +\ 50 \\ \hline \end{array}$$

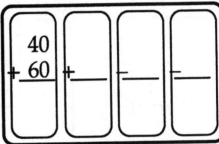

$$\begin{array}{r} 40 \\ +\ 60 \\ \hline \end{array}$$

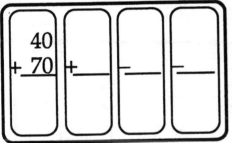

$$\begin{array}{r} 40 \\ +\ 70 \\ \hline \end{array}$$

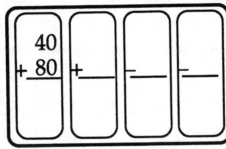

$$\begin{array}{r} 40 \\ +\ 80 \\ \hline \end{array}$$

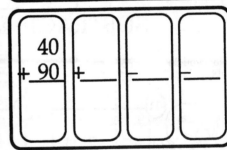

$$\begin{array}{r} 40 \\ +\ 90 \\ \hline \end{array}$$

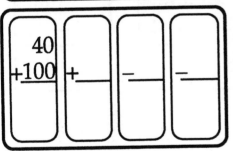

$$\begin{array}{r} 40 \\ +100 \\ \hline \end{array}$$

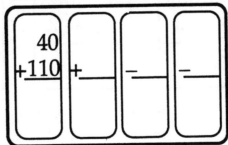

$$\begin{array}{r} 40 \\ +110 \\ \hline \end{array}$$

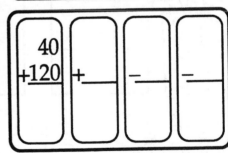

$$\begin{array}{r} 40 \\ +120 \\ \hline \end{array}$$

review

40 + 70 =	80 + 40 =	140 − 40 =	160 − 120 =
40 + 100 =	90 + 40 =	100 − 40 =	130 − 90 =
40 + 80 =	70 + 40 =	120 − 40 =	120 − 80 =
40 + 90 =	100 + 40 =	90 − 40 =	140 − 100 =
40 + 110 =	110 + 40 =	110 − 40 =	110 − 70 =
40 + 120 =	120 + 40 =	130 − 40 =	150 − 110 =

ADD   REGROUP FIRST then work these problems from right to left.

"First you do addition....."

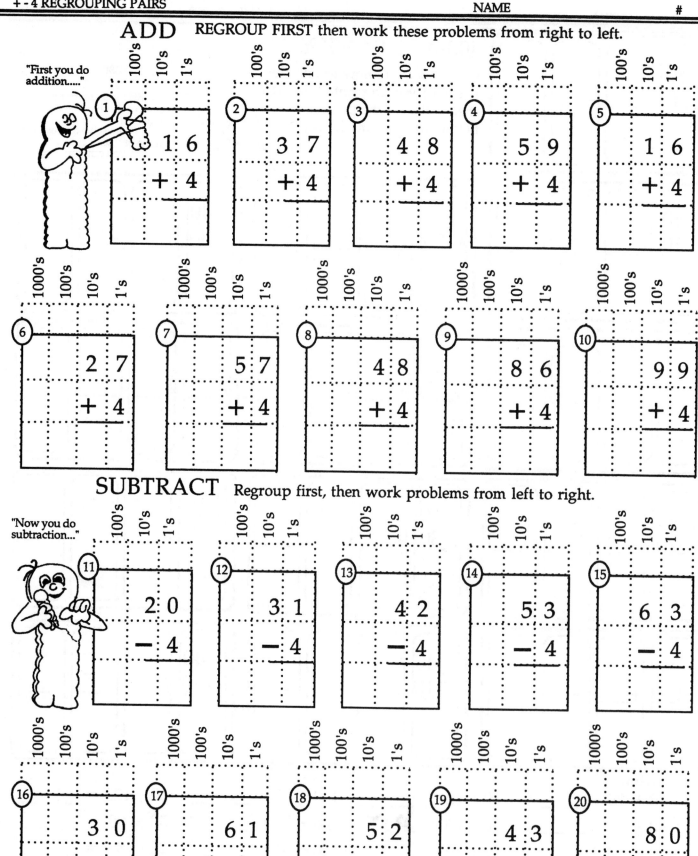

	100's	10's	1's
(1)		1	6
		+	4

	100's	10's	1's
(2)		3	7
		+	4

	100's	10's	1's
(3)		4	8
		+	4

	100's	10's	1's
(4)		5	9
		+	4

	100's	10's	1's
(5)		1	6
		+	4

	1000's	100's	10's	1's
(6)			2	7
			+	4

	1000's	100's	10's	1's
(7)			5	7
			+	4

	1000's	100's	10's	1's
(8)			4	8
			+	4

	1000's	100's	10's	1's
(9)			8	6
			+	4

	1000's	100's	10's	1's
(10)			9	9
			+	4

SUBTRACT   Regroup first, then work problems from left to right.

"Now you do subtraction..."

	100's	10's	1's
(11)		2	0
		−	4

	100's	10's	1's
(12)		3	1
		−	4

	100's	10's	1's
(13)		4	2
		−	4

	100's	10's	1's
(14)		5	3
		−	4

	100's	10's	1's
(15)		6	3
		−	4

	1000's	100's	10's	1's
(16)			3	0
			−	4

	1000's	100's	10's	1's
(17)			6	1
			−	4

	1000's	100's	10's	1's
(18)			5	2
			−	4

	1000's	100's	10's	1's
(19)			4	3
			−	4

	1000's	100's	10's	1's
(20)			8	0
			−	4

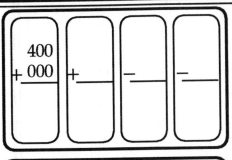

400 FACT FAMILY

Use what you know to find the answer for each printed problem, then write all the problems that belong to the same family.

Circle any regrouping pair of numbers, add or subtract.

"I'm glad I don't have to count things to add hundreds. It would take all day."

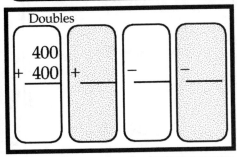

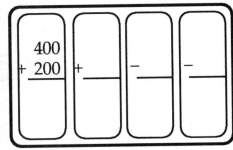

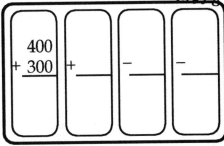

Doubles

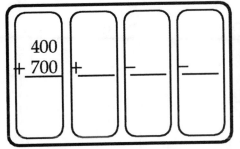

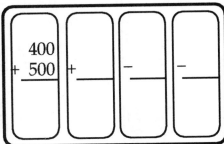

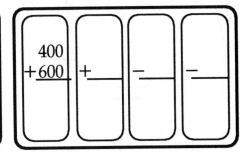

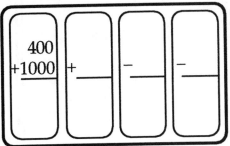

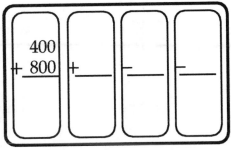

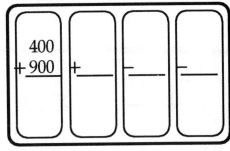

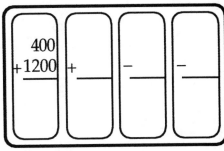

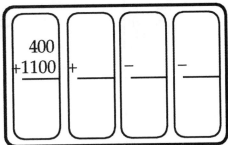

review

400 + 700 = _____	800 + 400 = _____	1400 − 400 = _____	1600 − 1200 = _____
400 + 1000 = _____	900 + 400 = _____	1000 − 400 = _____	1300 − 900 = _____
400 + 800 = _____	700 + 400 = _____	1200 − 400 = _____	1200 − 800 = _____
400 + 900 = _____	1000 + 400 = _____	900 − 400 = _____	1400 − 1000 = _____
400 + 1100 = _____	1100 + 400 = _____	1100 − 400 = _____	1100 − 700 = _____
400 + 1200 = _____	1200 + 400 = _____	1300 − 400 = _____	1500 − 1100 = _____

POWER PAGE

I know that 4 + 5 = 9
Therefore: I know

5 +4	4 +5	9 -5	9 -4
9	9	4	5

ADD

A.
5	4	50	40	55	44	54	45	500	400	550	440	505
+4	+5	+40	+50	+44	+55	+45	+54	+400	+500	+440	+550	+404

B.
404	405	540	450	555	554	445	545	454	455	544
+505	+504	+450	+540	+444	+445	+554	+454	+545	+544	+455

SUBTRACT

C.
9	9	90	90	99	99	99	99	900	900	990	990	909
-4	-5	-40	-50	-44	-45	-54	-55	-400	-500	-440	-550	-404

D.
909	909	990	990	999	999	999	999	999	999	999	999
-505	-405	-540	-450	-555	-444	-554	-445	-454	-545	-544	-455

> Two students work together. One reads the problems, the other gives the answers from memory. Take turns reading the problems.

Watch the signs!

+ - 4 THINKER SHEET

0 +4 4	4 +6 10	13 -9 4	4 +3 7	4 +10 14	14 -4 10	7 +4 11	4 -1 3
14 -10 4	6 -2 4	10 -6 4	6 +4 10	12 -4 8	5 -4 1	11 +4 15	11 -7 4
16 -12 4	15 -11 4	9 +4 13	9 -4 5	4 +7 11	6 -4 2	4 +8 12	4 -3 1
15 -4 11	4 +4 8	12 -8 4	4 +1 5	8 -4 4	5 -1 4	4 +2 6	16 -12 4
90 -50 40	40 -10 30	40 +40 80	40 +50 90	130 -40 90	40 +110 150	160 +40 200	40 -20 20
120 +40 160	100 -40 60	80 +40 120	10 +40 50	50 +40 90	70 +40 110	110 -40 70	40 -40 0
110 -70 40	300 +400 700	400 +900 1300 Say: thirteen hundred.	800 -400 400	400 +1200 1600 Say: sixteen hundred.	1000 +400 1400 Say: fourteen hundred.	700 -300 400	400 +100 500

LESSON PLANS FOR TEACHING + - 5

1. Complete the + - 5 PENNY PAGES. If students are doing well on the other written work, it may not be necessary to use the manipulatives for this page.

2. Dance and say + and - problems with the # 5 WRAP-UP RAP tapes .

3. Practice with the LEARNING WRAP-UPS for add 5.

4. Write the COMMUTATIVE PARTNERS and SUBTRACTION BUDDIES, answers, p. 93. (Cut up a set of blank problems and hide them around the room during recess or lunch. When the students come back, have them find a problem, bring it to you and tell the answer. Initial the problem. They go back to find another one. The objective is to find and answer as many problems as they can.)

5. Do the + - 5 FACT FAMILY worksheet, p. 94.

6. Do the + 5 WORD PROBLEMS, p. 95.

7. Do + - 50 FACT FAMILY worksheet, p. 96.

8. Work on the +5 REGROUPING, p. 97
   - TALK ABOUT which number pairs need to be regrouped.
     ADDITION regrouping pairs are 5 + 5, 5 + 6, 5 + 7, 5 + 8, and 5 + 9 and their COMMUTATIVE PARTNERS . Have students look for the pairs that will need to be regrouped. Problems 16-20 have regrouping in the 10's column. Explain that the process is the same as regrouping in the 1's column. Give students an opportunity to solve a problem on their own. Then give help where needed.

     When all of the regrouping pairs have been identified, ask if students could work the problems from left to right.   Some students will prefer to go right to left. Tell them it is OK. But it will help them later if they can work the problem from left to right.

     Use the DOLLAR, DIME and PENNY Chart to help them increase their understanding of regrouping.

9. Do the - 5 REGROUPING worksheet, p. 98. Have students get the problems ready by identifying the number pairs that need to be regrouped, then work the problems from left to right.

10. Do + - 500 FACT FAMILY worksheet, p. 99.

11. Do the 5+8 POWER PAGE, p.100. There are not as many problems to do as on other POWER PAGES. Tell students this is easier than the REGROUPING PAGES. Work the bottom row of problems on the chalkboard if necessary. Be certain students have their DDP chart out to help them understand the problems.

12. Pair up to do the + - 5 THINKER SHEET, p. 101.

13. SEND HOME four Wrap-ups. + 4, - 4, + 5, - 5. Suggest students have WRAP-OFFS with their parents.

NEXT DAY

- Have a WRAP-OFF with the 4 and 5 Wrap-ups.

- Give the + - 5 QUICK QUIZ, p. 23 and mark the "HERE'S WHAT I KNOW" Chart.

+ 5 PENNY PAGE   Always start at 1 when covering the number circles to solve problems.

(1) (2) (3) (4) (5) (6) (7) (8) (9) **10**

(11) (12) (13) (14) (15) (16) (17) (18) (19) **20**

A.   Use pennies or discs to solve these problems.

1 + 5 =	11 + 5 =
6 + 5 =	
2 + 5 =	12 + 5 =
7 + 5 =	
3 + 5 =	13 + 5 =
8 + 5 =	
4 + 5 =	14 + 5 =
9 + 5 =	
5 + 5 =	15 + 5 =
10 + 5 =	

Each student should have 20 pennies. Make certain all the problems in section A are correct. Trade 10 pennies for a dime when appropriate.

Use the #5 Addition Learning Wrap-up, and do it several times. Be sure to say the problems and answers aloud.

Remind students of the commutative properties of addition, before they do the set of problems. Fold papers in half and do the problems in section B.

Do the #5 Addition Learning Wrap-up and mark a square each time you do it correctly.

Use pennies to solve these problems if necessary.

1 +5	2 +5	3 +5	4 +5	5 +5	6 +5
7 +5	8 +5	9 +5	10 +5	11 +5	12 +5
5 +1	5 +4	5 +10	5 +7	5 +8	5 +5
5 +12	5 +2	5 +3	5 +6	5 +9	5 +11

B.

91   © Learning Wrap-ups Inc. 1997

– 5 PENNY PAGE

Always start at 1 when covering the number circles to solve problems. To take away or subtract, remove discs or pennies starting from the last circle you covered.

1	2	3	4	5	6	7	8	9	**10**
11	12	13	14	15	16	17	18	19	**20**

Do the #5 Subtraction Learning Wrap-up and mark a square each time you do it correctly.

☒ □ □ □ □ □ □ □ □ □

Use pennies to solve these problems if necessary.

5 − 5	6 − 5	7 − 5	8 − 5	9 − 5	**10** − 5
11 − 5	**12** − 5	**13** − 5	**14** − 5	**15** − 5	**16** − 5
5 − 5	**14** − 5	**13** − 5	**15** − 5	7 − 5	**12** − 5
6 − 5	**10** − 5	**17** − 5	8 − 5	**11** − 5	9 − 5

B.

A.

Use pennies or discs to solve these problems.

5 - 5 = □

10 - 5 = □　　15 - 5 = □

6 - 5 = □

11 - 5 = □　　16 - 5 = □

7 - 5 = □

12 - 5 = □　　17 - 5 = □

8 - 5 = □

13 - 5 = □　　18 - 5 = □

9 - 5 = □

14 - 5 = □　　19 - 5 = □

Each student should have 20 pennies and a dime. Be certain students have all the answers in section A correct. Emphasize that any number subtracted from itself equals 0. Wrap-ups do not cover 0's. Make sure students understand it now.

Do #5 Subtraction Learning Wrap-up, saying problems and answers aloud at least 10 times. Then fold paper and do section B as fast as possible.

COMMUTATIVE PARTNERS		SUBTRACTION BUDDIES	
1+5=____	5+1=____	6-5=____	6-1=____
2+5=____	5+2=____	7-5=____	7-2=____
3+5=____	5+3=____	8-5=____	8-3=____
4+5=____	5+4=____	9-5=____	9-4=____
5+5=____	5+5=____	10-5=____	10-5=____
6+5=____	5+6=____	11-5=____	11-6=____
7+5=____	5+7=____	12-5=____	12-7=____
8+5=____	5+8=____	13-5=____	13-8=____
9+5=____	5+9=____	14-5=____	14-9=____
10+5=____	5+10=____	15-5=____	15-10=____
11+5=____	5+11=____	16-5=____	16-11=____
12+5=____	5+12=____	17-5=____	17-12=____

5 FACT FAMILY

"I'm on my way to winding up the fives."

Use what you know to find the answer for each printed problem, then write all the problems that belong to the same family.

Circle all the number pairs that need to be regrouped. Be sure to circle the subtraction regrouping pairs also.

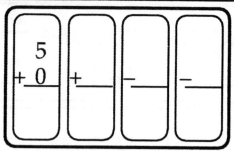

$5 + 0$

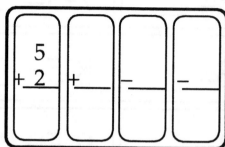

$5 + 1$ $5 + 2$ $5 + 3$

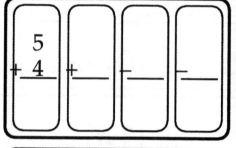 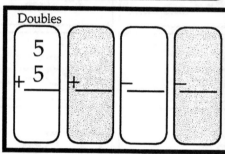 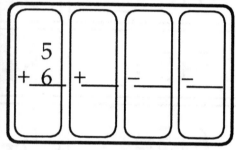

$5 + 4$ Doubles $5 + 5$ $5 + 6$

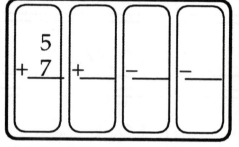 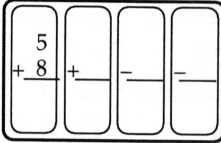 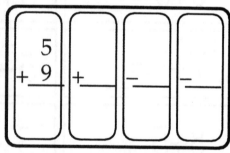

$5 + 7$ $5 + 8$ $5 + 9$

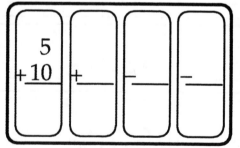 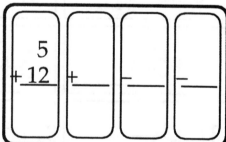

$5 + 10$ $5 + 11$ $5 + 12$

review

$5 + 7 =$ ____	$8 + 5 =$ ____	$14 - 5 =$ ____	$17 - 12 =$ ____
$5 + 10 =$ ____	$9 + 5 =$ ____	$10 - 5 =$ ____	$14 - 9 =$ ____
$5 + 8 =$ ____	$7 + 5 =$ ____	$12 - 5 =$ ____	$13 - 8 =$ ____
$5 + 9 =$ ____	$10 + 5 =$ ____	$9 - 5 =$ ____	$15 - 10 =$ ____
$5 + 11 =$ ____	$11 + 5 =$ ____	$11 - 5 =$ ____	$12 - 7 =$ ____
$5 + 12 =$ ____	$12 + 5 =$ ____	$13 - 5 =$ ____	$16 - 11 =$ ____

AS A MATTER OF FACTS.....IT WAS FUNNY!

It was raining outside. No one could go out. _____ asked if we could tell jokes or funny stories during our break. We decided to keep a chart about it, then write word problems. We also can write the COMMUTATIVE PARNERS and SUBTRACTION BUDDIES to go with each problem.

1. _____ said that 6 students told "Knock knock" jokes about animals. _____ said 5 others told "Knock, knock" jokes about people. How many students told "Knock, knock" jokes?

2. 5 students found funny joke books at the library. 7 other students found books about funny tall tales. How many students found something funny at the library?

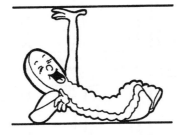

3. _____ used the stop watch to find out how long it took to tell a joke. _____ took 9 seconds. _____ took 5 seconds. What was the total seconds for both jokes?

4. 3 students drew funny animals on the chalkboard. 5 students drew funny faces on pieces of paper. How many students did drawings?

5. When _____went home, he clipped the cartoons out of the newspaper. On Monday there were 5. On Tuesday there were 8. How many cartoons in two days?

6. Everybody laughed for 5 seconds after _____'s joke. They laughed for 4 seconds after _____'s joke. How many seconds of laughter did that add up to?

50 FACT FAMILY

Use what you know to find the answer for each printed problem, then write all the problems that belong to the same family.

Circle the regrouping pairs for add and subtract.

"Don't you just love being so smart?" ♥

♥
♥
♥

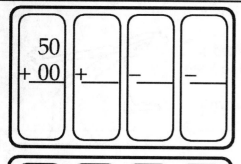
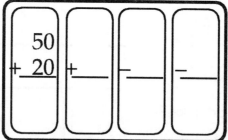
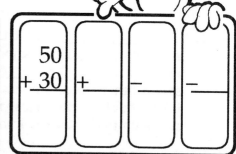

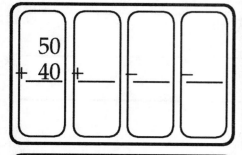
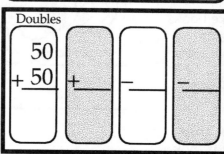
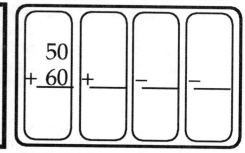

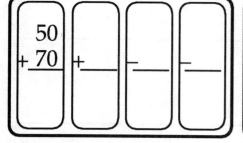

Doubles

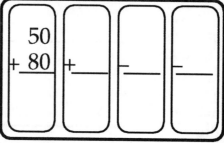
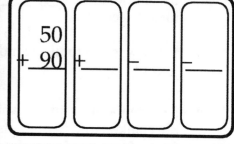

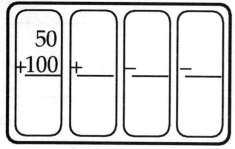
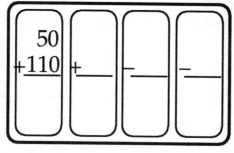
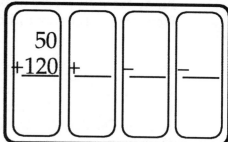

review

50 + 70 = _____	80 + 50 = _____	140 − 50 = _____	170 − 120 = _____
50 + 100 = _____	90 + 50 = _____	100 − 50 = _____	140 − 90 = _____
50 + 80 = _____	70 + 50 = _____	120 − 50 = _____	130 − 80 = _____
50 + 90 = _____	100 + 50 = _____	90 − 50 = _____	150 − 100 = _____
50 + 110 = _____	110 + 50 = _____	110 − 50 = _____	120 − 70 = _____
50 + 120 = _____	120 + 50 = _____	130 − 50 = _____	160 − 110 = _____

Use the Dollar, Dime and Penny Chart to help understand these problems.
Can you regroup first then add from left to right?

"I can polish these off in a few minutes."

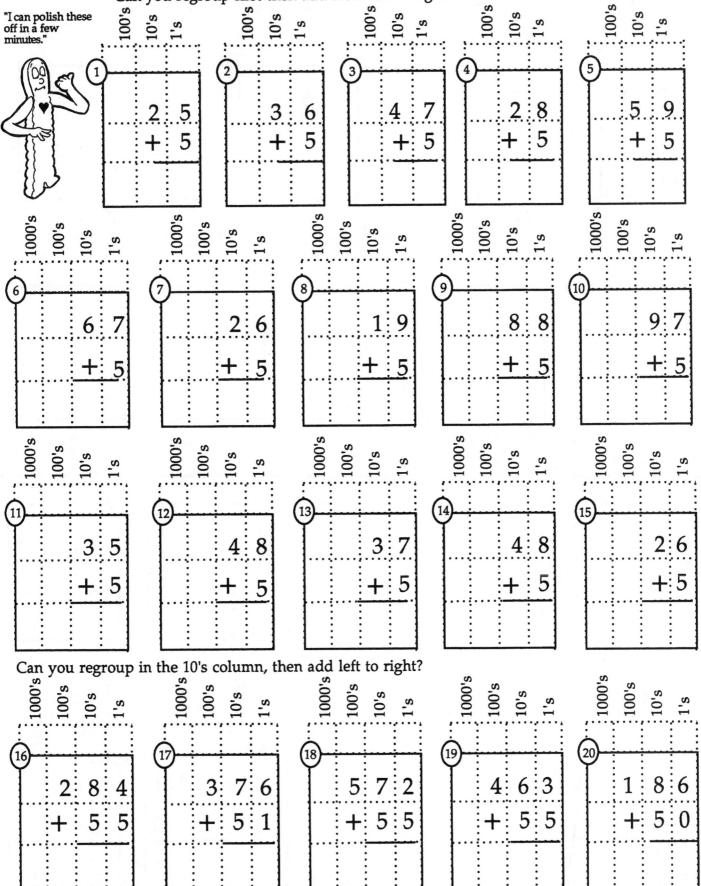

1.
$$\begin{array}{r} 2\ 5 \\ +\ 5 \\ \hline \end{array}$$

2.
$$\begin{array}{r} 3\ 6 \\ +\ 5 \\ \hline \end{array}$$

3.
$$\begin{array}{r} 4\ 7 \\ +\ 5 \\ \hline \end{array}$$

4.
$$\begin{array}{r} 2\ 8 \\ +\ 5 \\ \hline \end{array}$$

5.
$$\begin{array}{r} 5\ 9 \\ +\ 5 \\ \hline \end{array}$$

6.
$$\begin{array}{r} 6\ 7 \\ +\ 5 \\ \hline \end{array}$$

7.
$$\begin{array}{r} 2\ 6 \\ +\ 5 \\ \hline \end{array}$$

8.
$$\begin{array}{r} 1\ 9 \\ +\ 5 \\ \hline \end{array}$$

9.
$$\begin{array}{r} 8\ 8 \\ +\ 5 \\ \hline \end{array}$$

10.
$$\begin{array}{r} 9\ 7 \\ +\ 5 \\ \hline \end{array}$$

11.
$$\begin{array}{r} 3\ 5 \\ +\ 5 \\ \hline \end{array}$$

12.
$$\begin{array}{r} 4\ 8 \\ +\ 5 \\ \hline \end{array}$$

13.
$$\begin{array}{r} 3\ 7 \\ +\ 5 \\ \hline \end{array}$$

14.
$$\begin{array}{r} 4\ 8 \\ +\ 5 \\ \hline \end{array}$$

15.
$$\begin{array}{r} 2\ 6 \\ +\ 5 \\ \hline \end{array}$$

Can you regroup in the 10's column, then add left to right?

16.
$$\begin{array}{r} 2\ 8\ 4 \\ +\ 5\ 5 \\ \hline \end{array}$$

17.
$$\begin{array}{r} 3\ 7\ 6 \\ +\ 5\ 1 \\ \hline \end{array}$$

18.
$$\begin{array}{r} 5\ 7\ 2 \\ +\ 5\ 5 \\ \hline \end{array}$$

19.
$$\begin{array}{r} 4\ 6\ 3 \\ +\ 5\ 5 \\ \hline \end{array}$$

20.
$$\begin{array}{r} 1\ 8\ 6 \\ +\ 5\ 0 \\ \hline \end{array}$$

Use the Dollars, Dime and Penny Chart to help solve these problems.
Regroup first then subtract from left to right.

"When I can regroup, the sky's the limit!"

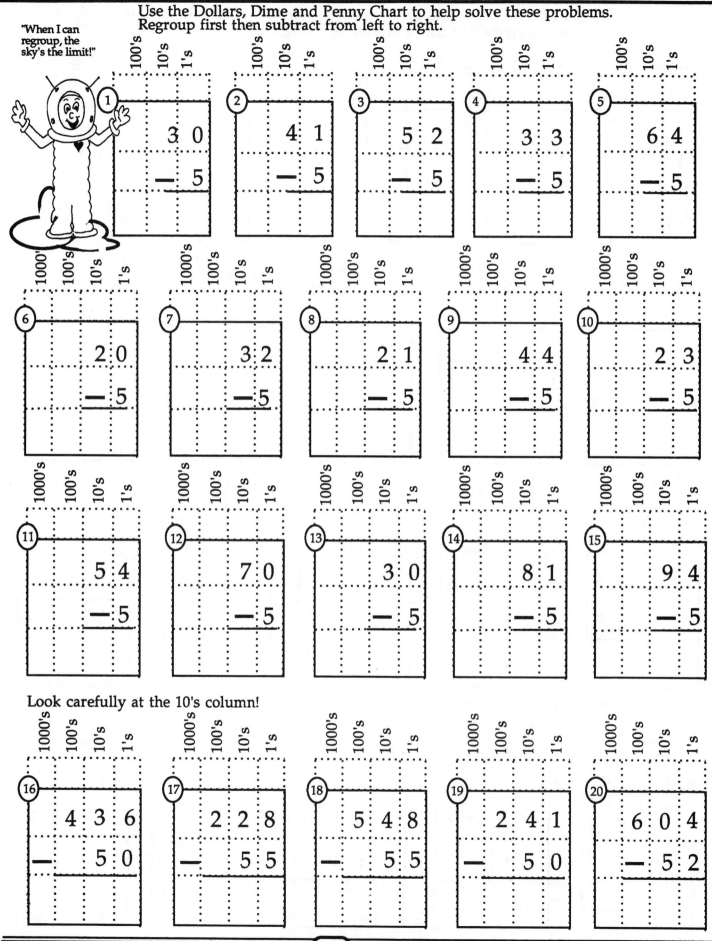

	100's	10's	1's
1		3	0
		−	5

	100's	10's	1's
2		4	1
		−	5

	100's	10's	1's
3		5	2
		−	5

	100's	10's	1's
4		3	3
		−	5

	100's	10's	1's
5		6	4
		−	5

	1000's	100's	10's	1's
6			2	0
			−	5

	1000's	100's	10's	1's
7			3	2
			−	5

	1000's	100's	10's	1's
8			2	1
			−	5

	1000's	100's	10's	1's
9			4	4
			−	5

	1000's	100's	10's	1's
10			2	3
			−	5

	1000's	100's	10's	1's
11			5	4
			−	5

	1000's	100's	10's	1's
12			7	0
			−	5

	1000's	100's	10's	1's
13			3	0
			−	5

	1000's	100's	10's	1's
14			8	1
			−	5

	1000's	100's	10's	1's
15			9	4
			−	5

Look carefully at the 10's column!

	1000's	100's	10's	1's
16		4	3	6
		−	5	0

	1000's	100's	10's	1's
17		2	2	8
		−	5	5

	1000's	100's	10's	1's
18		5	4	8
		−	5	5

	1000's	100's	10's	1's
19		2	4	1
		−	5	0

	1000's	100's	10's	1's
20		6	0	4
		−	5	2

500 FACT FAMILY

Use what you know to find the answer for each printed problem, then write all the problems that belong to the same family.

Circle the regrouping pairs.

"Everything
is simple
when you
know how
to do it"

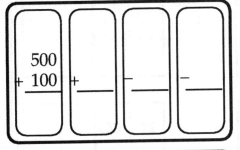

500
+ 000

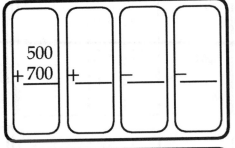

500
+ 100

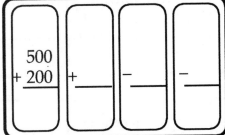

500
+ 200

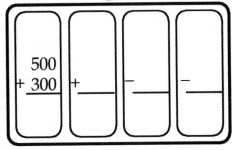

500
+ 300

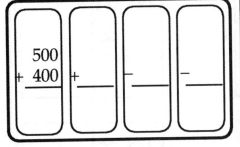

500
+ 400

Doubles

500
+ 500

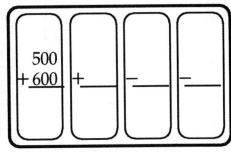

500
+ 600

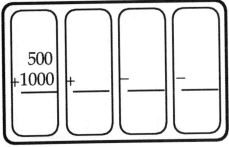

500
+ 700

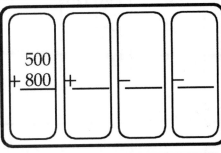

500
+ 800

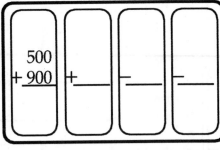

500
+ 900

500
+1000

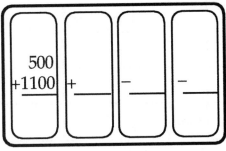

500
+1100

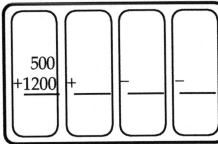

500
+1200

review

500 + 700 = ___	800 + 500 = ___	1400 − 500 = ___	1700 − 1200 = ___
500 +1000= ___	900 + 500 = ___	1000 − 500 = ___	1400 − 900 = ___
500 + 800 = ___	700 + 500 = ___	1200 − 500 = ___	1300 − 800 = ___
500 + 900 = ___	1000+ 500 = ___	900 − 500 = ___	1500 − 1000 = ___
500 +1100= ___	1100+ 500 = ___	1100 − 500 = ___	1200 − 700 = ___
500 +1200= ___	1200+ 500 = ___	1300 − 500 = ___	1600 − 1100 = ___

WATCH THE SIGNS! Mark the regroupers from right to left if you need to. Then add or subtract from left to right.

$$\begin{array}{r} 58 \\ +\,85 \\ \hline \end{array} \qquad \begin{array}{r} 888 \\ -\,55 \\ \hline \end{array} \qquad \begin{array}{r} 138 \\ -\,85 \\ \hline \end{array}$$

$$\begin{array}{r} 55 \\ +\,88 \\ \hline \end{array} \qquad \begin{array}{r} 583 \\ +\,8 \\ \hline \end{array} \qquad \begin{array}{r} 585 \\ +\,58 \\ \hline \end{array}$$

$$\begin{array}{r} 88 \\ +\,55 \\ \hline \end{array} \qquad \begin{array}{r} 553 \\ -\,5 \\ \hline \end{array} \qquad \begin{array}{r} 855 \\ +\,88 \\ \hline \end{array}$$

$$\begin{array}{r} 5 \\ +\,8 \\ \hline \end{array} \qquad \begin{array}{r} 13 \\ -\,8 \\ \hline \end{array} \qquad \begin{array}{r} 558 \\ +\,85 \\ \hline \end{array}$$

$$\begin{array}{r} 8 \\ +\,5 \\ \hline \end{array} \qquad \begin{array}{r} 13 \\ -\,5 \\ \hline \end{array} \qquad \begin{array}{r} 138 \\ +\,55 \\ \hline \end{array}$$

(Place value column headers in each box, from right to left: 1's, 10's, 100's, 1000's)

"It's best when it's in your head."

Two students work together. One reads the problems, the other gives the answers from memory. Take turns reading the problems.

Watch the signs!

A.

| $\begin{array}{r}12\\-5\\\hline 7\end{array}$ | $\begin{array}{r}4\\+5\\\hline 9\end{array}$ | $\begin{array}{r}14\\-9\\\hline 5\end{array}$ | $\begin{array}{r}5\\+7\\\hline 12\end{array}$ | $\begin{array}{r}5\\+5\\\hline 10\end{array}$ | $\begin{array}{r}8\\-5\\\hline 3\end{array}$ | $\begin{array}{r}10\\-5\\\hline 5\end{array}$ | $\begin{array}{r}17\\-12\\\hline 5\end{array}$ |

B.

| $\begin{array}{r}0\\+5\\\hline 5\end{array}$ | $\begin{array}{r}5\\+6\\\hline 11\end{array}$ | $\begin{array}{r}13\\-5\\\hline 8\end{array}$ | $\begin{array}{r}7\\+5\\\hline 12\end{array}$ | $\begin{array}{r}5\\-5\\\hline 0\end{array}$ | $\begin{array}{r}16\\-5\\\hline 11\end{array}$ | $\begin{array}{r}11\\+5\\\hline 16\end{array}$ | $\begin{array}{r}5\\-1\\\hline 4\end{array}$ |

C.

| $\begin{array}{r}15\\-5\\\hline 10\end{array}$ | $\begin{array}{r}9\\+5\\\hline 14\end{array}$ | $\begin{array}{r}15\\-10\\\hline 5\end{array}$ | $\begin{array}{r}5\\+5\\\hline 10\end{array}$ | $\begin{array}{r}10\\-5\\\hline 5\end{array}$ | $\begin{array}{r}6\\-5\\\hline 1\end{array}$ | $\begin{array}{r}8\\-3\\\hline 5\end{array}$ | $\begin{array}{r}5\\-4\\\hline 1\end{array}$ |

D.

| $\begin{array}{r}7\\-2\\\hline 5\end{array}$ | $\begin{array}{r}17\\-5\\\hline 12\end{array}$ | $\begin{array}{r}13\\-8\\\hline 5\end{array}$ | $\begin{array}{r}5\\+1\\\hline 6\end{array}$ | $\begin{array}{r}5\\+2\\\hline 7\end{array}$ | $\begin{array}{r}5\\+10\\\hline 15\end{array}$ | $\begin{array}{r}5\\+4\\\hline 9\end{array}$ | $\begin{array}{r}5\\-3\\\hline 2\end{array}$ |

E.

| $\begin{array}{r}120\\-70\\\hline 50\end{array}$ | $\begin{array}{r}80\\+50\\\hline 130\end{array}$ | $\begin{array}{r}110\\-60\\\hline 50\end{array}$ | $\begin{array}{r}90\\-40\\\hline 50\end{array}$ | $\begin{array}{r}50\\+10\\\hline 60\end{array}$ | $\begin{array}{r}50\\+110\\\hline 160\end{array}$ | $\begin{array}{r}50\\-40\\\hline 10\end{array}$ | $\begin{array}{r}50\\-20\\\hline 30\end{array}$ |

F.

| $\begin{array}{r}120\\+50\\\hline 170\end{array}$ | $\begin{array}{r}30\\+50\\\hline 80\end{array}$ | $\begin{array}{r}10\\+50\\\hline 60\end{array}$ | $\begin{array}{r}110\\-50\\\hline 60\end{array}$ | $\begin{array}{r}50\\-50\\\hline 0\end{array}$ | $\begin{array}{r}50\\+80\\\hline 130\end{array}$ | $\begin{array}{r}140\\-50\\\hline 90\end{array}$ | $\begin{array}{r}60\\-10\\\hline 50\end{array}$ |

G.

| $\begin{array}{r}600\\+500\\\hline 1100\end{array}$ | $\begin{array}{r}900\\-500\\\hline 400\end{array}$ | $\begin{array}{r}1600\\-1100\\\hline 500\end{array}$ | $\begin{array}{r}500\\+300\\\hline 800\end{array}$ | $\begin{array}{r}100\\+500\\\hline 600\end{array}$ | $\begin{array}{r}700\\+500\\\hline 1200\end{array}$ | $\begin{array}{r}500\\+1200\\\hline 1700\end{array}$ | $\begin{array}{r}500\\+900\\\hline 1400\end{array}$ |

LESSON PLANS COMBINATIONS OF 10 and DOING DOUBLES

1. Give the PRE/POST TEST, p. 23, for the first five sets of facts. It will tell you if there needs to be any review up to this point.

2. Give the PRE/POST TEST, p. 24.
   Before giving the test, TALK ABOUT the things the students have learned. They will be able to apply much of what they have learned already to the rest of the facts. Explain that you are giving a test on the 6, 7, 8, 9 and 10 facts so they can see what they have already learned. Explain how important it is for them to think about COMMUTATIVE PARTNERS and SUBTRACTION BUDDIES. Allow extra time. Walk about the classroom to observe how the students are doing. Have students circle the problems for which they did not have an answer. Then have them correct their own papers. Tell them you are not going to keep a record of their scores, but you will collect the papers. This will help you know which facts need the most work.

   • • • • •

3. TALK ABOUT the importance of knowing all the combinations of 10. If the COMMUTATIVE PARTNERS are taken into consideration, all the combinations of 10 have been taught. It is important for students to know ways to use this knowledge. Do THINKING COMBINATIONS OF 10, p. 103. (Print 2 copies per student.)   When students show proficiency with combinations of 10, discuss the information on LOOKING FOR COMBINATIONS OF 10, p.104.

4. Drill orally, adding 10 to single-digit numbers, then two-digit numbers. Write some problems on the board and have students "think" the answers, then give them orally. If students understand the importance of the number 10, they can use it to add to, or subtract from. Some examples: "If 6 + 10 is 16, how much is 6 + 9?" "If 22 + 10 = 32, how much is 22 + 9?" Use all of the time necessary to be certain students understand the number 10, how to add it, how to subtract it and how to use it as a friend to help solve problems.
   Practice with the #10 Addition WRAP-UP.

5. Have students write problems using a 10 on a copy of the REGROUPING BLANK PAGE, p. 28.

   • • • • •

6. Talk to the students about knowing the DOUBLE COMBINATIONS. Help them to understand that knowing all of the doubles can also become a base to add up to or count down from if they don't know a certain fact.

7. Learning Wrap-ups do not cover doubles separately because they are learned along with each set of facts. However, it will be an advantage to the students to learn the last 4 sets of doubles at this point.

8. Write the 4 doubles they have not learned on the chalkboard (6+6, 7+7, 8+8 and 9+9.) Ask students if they can use anything they already know to help them find the answers to these 4 problems. Drill the doubles orally. Give each student a copy of p. 32, ORDERED FACTS. Color all of the problems that are doubles. *During the next several days, ask for oral answers to doubles facts everyt ime you think of it.*

9. Students should enjoy doing the DOUBLES SCRAMBLE PAGE, p. 105. Make 2 copies for each student. Have them work one in class, then assign one to do at home.

10. TALK ABOUT what they have learned.   Do some oral drill to help them understand the importance of knowing the doubles. Ask some questions like the ones below:
    "I know that 7+7 is 14, how much is 7+8?"   "I know that 6+6 is 12, how much is 6+7?"
    "I know that 9+9 is 18, how much is 9+8?"   "I know that 8+8 is 16, how much is 8+7?"

11. Have students pair up to play the DOUBLES GAME, p. 106.

THINKING COMBINATIONS OF 10

Write in the numbers that will total 10 as fast as you can. Use a timer to measure your speed.
Fold completed rows under before doing next row.

A.   3   9   __   5   2   6   10   7   4   8   5   10   7   1   9   4   2   8   3   6   time ___ min. ___ sec.

THINKING COMBINATIONS OF 10   NAME

B.   6   2   5   3   1   7   8   4   10   1   3   6   2   8   9   7   10   5   4   time ___ min. ___ sec.

THINKING COMBINATIONS OF 10   NAME

C.   1   4   7   2   8   10   3   9   5   6   10   2   1   5   3   4   9   6   8   7   time ___ min. ___ sec.

THINKING COMBINATIONS OF 10   NAME

D.   10   3   9   5   8   1   6   2   4   7   10   8   7   3   4   5   2   9   1   time ___ min. ___ sec.

THINKING COMBINATIONS OF 10   NAME

E.   2   5   8   3   6   4   7   10   1   9   2   5   3   1   4   8   7   10   6   9   time ___ min. ___ sec.

F.   Wrap the +10 LEARNING WRAP-UP. Mark a square each time you do it. ☒

103

© Learning Wrap-ups Inc. 1997

LOOKING FOR COMBINATIONS OF 10

Look for combinations of 10, then add the third number.

$$\begin{matrix} 6 \\ 4 \\ 6 \end{matrix} \quad \text{Think } 6+4 \quad =10+6=16$$

$$\begin{matrix} 4 \\ 7 \\ 3 \end{matrix} \quad \text{Think } 7+3 \quad =10+4=$$

$$\begin{matrix} 9 \\ 1 \\ 8 \end{matrix} \quad \text{Think } 9+1 \quad =10+8$$

$$\begin{matrix} 8 \\ 2 \\ 6 \end{matrix} \quad \text{Think } 8+2 \quad =10+6$$

$$\begin{matrix} 5 \\ 9 \\ 5 \end{matrix} =10+9=$$

$$\begin{matrix} 6 \\ 9 \\ 4 \end{matrix} =10+9=$$

$$\begin{matrix} 7 \\ 5 \\ 3 \end{matrix} =10+5=$$

$$\begin{matrix} 9 \\ 4 \\ 1 \end{matrix} =10+4=$$

Draw the lines to show which two numbers you choose to add first mentally, then add the third number and write the answer below the problem.

A.

8	6	3	9	5	2	3	4	2	4
5	7	7	8	5	8	8	6	2	6
2	4	1	1	7	5	7	9	6	9

B.

9	6	5	3	5	1	9	2	8	2
1	2	3	2	9	4	5	8	9	8
1	4	7	8	5	6	5	8	1	4

C.

7	4	8	2	4	3	7	9	1	6
4	6	2	6	5	6	8	1	7	4
3	9	3	4	6	7	2	6	9	8

D.

7	6	5	4	8	4	3	8	2	1
3	7	5	1	2	3	7	5	7	9
5	3	1	9	7	6	2	5	8	3

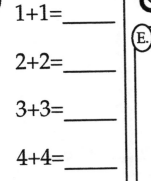

"Double, double,
Who caused the
trouble?"

We will have a reason to celebrate if you can find all the add facts that are doubles. Someone got into the computer and scrambled this page. How many problems can you answer?

number of problems

A. You already know these!

1	2	3	4	5	10	11	12
+1	+2	+3	+4	+5	+10	+11	+12

B. These 4 problems are all of the doubles that are left to learn.

6	7	8	9
+6	+7	+8	+9
12	14	16	18

C. 6 +6, 8 +8, 7 +7, 9 +9 (printed upside down)

D.
1+1=_____
2+2=_____
3+3=_____
4+4=_____
5+5=_____
10+10=_____
11+11=_____
12+12=_____
6+6=_____
7+7=_____
8+8=_____
9+9=_____

E. 9+9=_____ 7+7=_____

F.
6+6=_____
9+9=_____
7+7=_____

G. 14 −7 ____ 8 +8 ____

H. 8+8=_____

I. 18 −9 ____ 6 +6 ____

J. _____=9+9 _____=7+7

K. 8+8=_____ 6+6=_____

L. 16−8=_____

M. 7 +7 ____ 9 +9 ____ 6 +6 ____ 8 +8 ____

N.
12−6=_____
8+8=_____
7+7=_____
9+9=_____

O. 7 +7 ____ 16 −8 ____

P.
_____=9+9
_____=7+7
_____=8+8
_____=6+6

Q. 8 +8 ____ 6 +6 ____

R. 6 +6 ____ 8 +8 ____ 7 +7 ____ 9 +9 ____

S. 18−9=_____ 14−7=_____

T.
8+8=_____
6+6=_____
7+7=_____
9+9=_____

U. 9 +9 ____ 6 +6 ____ 7 +7 ____ 8 +8 ____

TOP THE DOUBLES

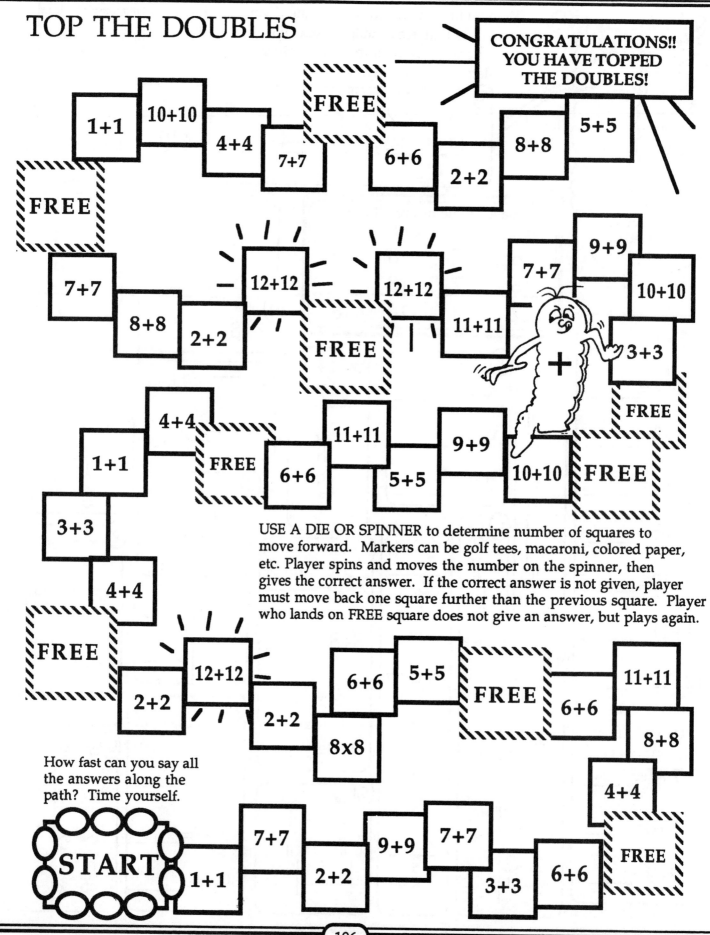

CONGRATULATIONS!!
YOU HAVE TOPPED
THE DOUBLES!

1+1   10+10   4+4   7+7   FREE   6+6   2+2   8+8   5+5

FREE

7+7   8+8   2+2   12+12   12+12   11+11   7+7   9+9   10+10   3+3

FREE   FREE

4+4   1+1   3+3   4+4   FREE   6+6   11+11   5+5   9+9   10+10   FREE

FREE

USE A DIE OR SPINNER to determine number of squares to move forward. Markers can be golf tees, macaroni, colored paper, etc. Player spins and moves the number on the spinner, then gives the correct answer. If the correct answer is not given, player must move back one square further than the previous square. Player who lands on FREE square does not give an answer, but plays again.

FREE   2+2   12+12   2+2   6+6   5+5   FREE   6+6   11+11   8+8   4+4   FREE

8x8

How fast can you say all the answers along the path? Time yourself.

START   1+1   7+7   2+2   9+9   7+7   3+3   6+6   FREE

LESSON PLANS FOR TEACHING + - 6

1. Do the + 6 and - 6 PENNY PAGES, pp. 108, 109. Practice with the LEARNING WRAP-UPS as indicated on the worksheets.
As students practice with the LEARNING WRAP-UPS, point out that they know at least 7 of the answers. Write the problems and answers for the facts they have not learned on the chalkboard. Tell students not to look at the answer if they can think of them in their head. After a few minutes, erase the answers.

2. Do the COMMUTATIVE PARTNERS and the SUBTRACTION BUDDIES, p. 110.

3. Play the - 6 WRAP-UP RAP. Have students dance and wrap the Wrap-up along with the rhythm.

4. Do the + - 6 FACT FAMILY worksheet, p. 111.

5. Do the + 6 WORD PROBLEMS, p. 112.

6. Practice with the - 6 LEARNING WRAP-UP.

7. Write several add, subtract problems using a 6 on the chalkboard. Have students do the problems on their DOLLAR, DIME and PENNY Chart and give the answers orally.

$$6+5 \quad 7+6 \quad 9+6 \quad 6+4 \quad 8+6 \quad 12-6 \quad 14-6 \quad 16-6 \quad 6+9$$

TALK ABOUT which of these problems they can do mentally. Explain they should always try to work the problems in their mind first. It will make them better math students.

$$62+61 \quad 52+65 \quad 66+4 \quad 66+40 \quad 66+6 \quad 67+60$$

THINK: $60+60+3=123$ $50+60+7=$ $60+10=$ $60+40+6=$ $60+12=$ $60+60+7=$

8. Do + - 60 FACT FAMILY, p. 113.

9. Work with the students on two REGROUPING pages for + - 6, pp. 114, 115. Write any problems that could cause trouble on the chalkboard and work as a class.

10. Practice writing the 6 facts on the RAPID WRITER worksheet, p. 116.

11. Do + - 600 FACT FAMILY, p. 117.

12. Do POWER PAGE using 6, 7, 3, with some regrouping, p. 118. Talk about saying 1761 as 17 hundred sixty one instead of one thousand, seven hundred. It will help them with mental math later.

13. Pair up students to do the + - 6 THINKER SHEET, p. 119. (Print a copy for every student.)

14. SEND HOME the + and - 6 LEARNING WRAP-UPS and a copy of the THINKER SHEET.

NEXT DAY

- Practice with the + - 6 WRAP-UPS.

- Give the + - 6 QUICK QUIZ, p. 23.

- Color in the "HERE'S WHAT I KNOW" chart. Count the number of problems left to learn.

- PRAISE, PRAISE, PRAISE.

+ 6 PENNY PAGE Always start at 1 when covering the number circles to solve problems.

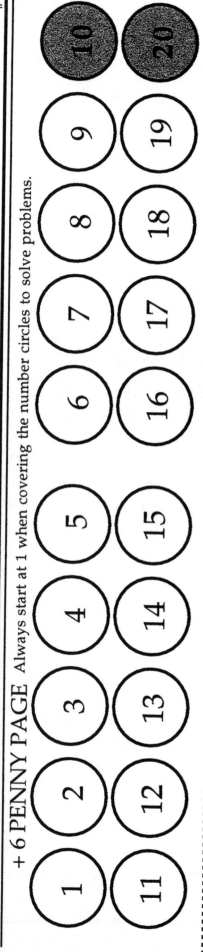

| 1 | 2 | 3 | 4 | 5 | 6 | 7 | 8 | 9 | 10 |
| 11 | 12 | 13 | 14 | 15 | 16 | 17 | 18 | 19 | 20 |

A.

Use pennies or discs to solve these problems.

$1 + 6 =$ ☐ $6 + 6 =$ ☐ $11 + 6 =$ ☐

$2 + 6 =$ ☐ $7 + 6 =$ ☐ $12 + 6 =$ ☐

$3 + 6 =$ ☐ $8 + 6 =$ ☐ $13 + 6 =$ ☐

$4 + 6 =$ ☐ $9 + 6 =$ ☐ $14 + 6 =$ ☐

$5 + 6 =$ ☐ $10 + 6 =$ ☐ $15 + 6 =$ ☐

Do the #6 Addition Learning Wrap-up and mark a square each time you do it correctly.

☒ ☐ ☐ ☐ ☐ ☐ ☐ ☐ ☐ ☐

B.

Use pennies to solve these problems if necessary.

$$1 + 6 \qquad 2 + 6 \qquad 3 + 6 \qquad 4 + 6 \qquad 5 + 6 \qquad 6 + 6$$

$$7 + 6 \qquad 8 + 6 \qquad 9 + 6 \qquad 10 + 6 \qquad 11 + 6 \qquad 12 + 6$$

$$6 + 1 \qquad 6 + 4 \qquad 6 + 10 \qquad 6 + 7 \qquad 6 + 8 \qquad 6 + 6$$

$$6 + 12 \qquad 6 + 2 \qquad 6 + 3 \qquad 6 + 6 \qquad 6 + 9 \qquad 6 + 5$$

$$6 + 11$$

Each student should have 20 pennies and a dime. Make certain all the problems in section A are correct. Exchange 10 pennies for a dime where appropriate.
Use the #6 Addition Learning Wrap-up, and do it at least 10 times.
Be sure to say the problems and answers aloud.
Remind students of the commutative properties of addition, before they do the set of problems in section B. Fold papers in half and do the problems in section B.

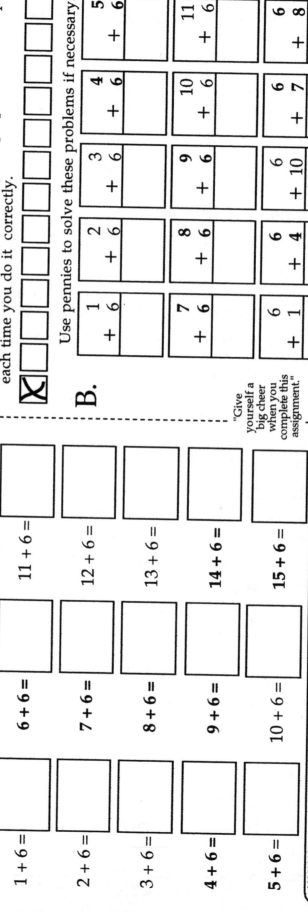

"Give yourself a big cheer when you complete this assignment."

108

USE PENNIES OR DISCS ON THE CIRCLES TO COMPLETE THESE PROBLEMS

NAME

#

- 6 PENNY PAGE
Always start at 1 when covering the number circles to solve problems.
To take away or subtract, remove discs or pennies starting from the last circle you covered.

| 1 | 2 | 3 | 4 | 5 | 6 | 7 | 8 | 9 | 10 |
| 11 | 12 | 13 | 14 | 15 | 16 | 17 | 18 | 19 | 20 |

A. Use pennies or discs to solve these problems.

6 - 6 = ☐   11 - 6 = ☐   16 - 6 = ☐

7 - 6 = ☐   12 - 6 = ☐   17 - 6 = ☐

8 - 6 = ☐   13 - 6 = ☐   18 - 6 = ☐

9 - 6 = ☐   14 - 6 = ☐   19 - 6 = ☐

10 - 6 = ☐   15 - 6 = ☐   20 - 6 = ☐

B. Do the #6 Subtraction Learning Wrap-up and mark a square each time you do it correctly.

☒ ☐ ☐ ☐ ☐ ☐ ☐ ☐ ☐ ☐ ☐

"A little extra practice on the darker number pairs will help you on the quiz later!

Close your eyes and repeat them in your mind, or have a friend say the problems for you to answer aloud."

Can you do these problems without using pennies or discs?

6 − 6	7 − 6	8 − 6	9 − 6	10 − 6	11 − 6
12 − 6	13 − 6	14 − 6	15 − 6	16 − 6	17 − 6
17 − 6	14 − 6	13 − 6	15 − 6	7 − 6	12 − 6
16 − 6	10 − 6	18 − 6	8 − 6	11 − 6	9 − 6

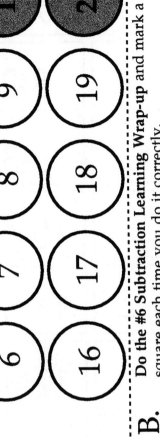

Each student should have 20 pennies. Be certain students have all the answers in section A correct. Emphasize that any number subtracted from itself equals 0. Wrap-ups do not cover 0's. Make sure students understand it now.

Do #6 Subtract Learning Wrap-up, saying problems and answers aloud at least 10 times. They then fold the paper and do section B for more practice.

COMMUTATIVE PARTNERS | SUBTRACTION BUDDIES

COMMUTATIVE PARTNERS		SUBTRACTION BUDDIES	
$1+6=$ ___	$6+1=$ ___	$7-6=$ ___	$7-1=$ ___
$2+6=$ ___	$6+2=$ ___	$8-6=$ ___	$8-2=$ ___
$3+6=$ ___	$6+3=$ ___	$9-6=$ ___	$9-3=$ ___
$4+6=$ ___	$6+4=$ ___	$10-6=$ ___	$10-4=$ ___
$5+6=$ ___	$6+5=$ ___	$11-6=$ ___	$11-5=$ ___
$6+6=$ ___	$6+6=$ ___	$12-6=$ ___	$12-6=$ ___
$7+6=$ ___	$6+7=$ ___	$13-6=$ ___	$13-7=$ ___
$8+6=$ ___	$6+8=$ ___	$14-6=$ ___	$14-8=$ ___
$9+6=$ ___	$6+9=$ ___	$15-6=$ ___	$15-9=$ ___
$10+6=$ ___	$6+10=$ ___	$16-6=$ ___	$16-10=$ ___
$11+6=$ ___	$6+11=$ ___	$17-6=$ ___	$17-11=$ ___
$12+6=$ ___	$6+12=$ ___	$18-6=$ ___	$18-12=$ ___

NAME _____ #

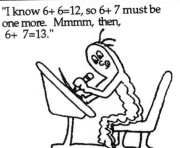

$$\begin{array}{r} 6 \\ +\ 0 \\ \hline \end{array}$$

6 FACT FAMILY

Use what you know to find the answer for each printed problem, then write all the problems that belong to the same family.

Circle the REGROUPING PAIRS?

Watch carefully, the fact families have been rearranged.

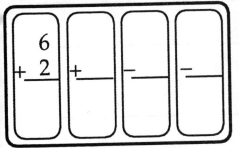

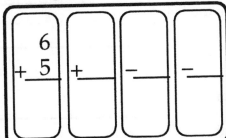

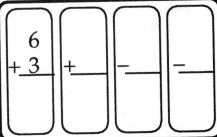

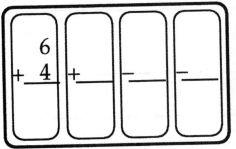

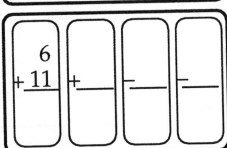

Doubles

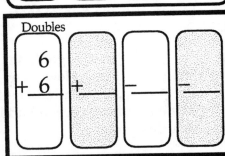

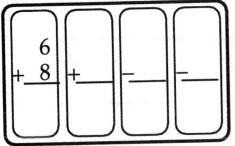

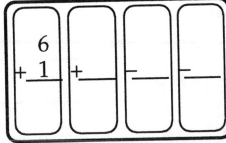

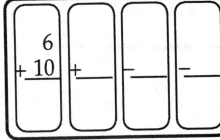

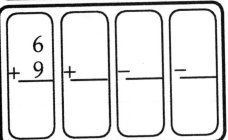

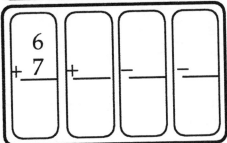

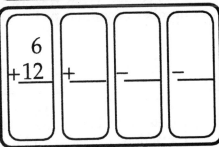

review

6 + 7 = _____	8 + 6 = _____	14 − 6 = _____	18 − 12 = _____
6 + 10 = _____	9 + 6 = _____	10 − 6 = _____	15 − 9 = _____
6 + 8 = _____	7 + 6 = _____	12 − 6 = _____	14 − 8 = _____
6 + 9 = _____	10 + 6 = _____	9 − 6 = _____	16 − 10 = _____
6 + 11 = _____	11 + 6 = _____	11 − 6 = _____	13 − 7 = _____
6 + 12 = _____	12 + 6 = _____	13 − 6 = _____	17 − 11 = _____

OUR PET PROJECT... MATH

In class we talked about our pets. We kept a chart showing all of the pets, then wrote math problems. We knew that if we could solve the original problem, we could do at least 3 more problems using the same numbers.

1. _____ counted the students who had pet dogs. There were 8. 6 students had cats. What was the total number of dogs and cats?

2. _____ said she had a stuffed giraffe and a stuffed elephant for her pets. _____ had 6 teddy bears. How many stuffed animals did the two of them have?

3. _____had 8 goldfish, but the cat ate 2 of them. How many were left? Can you do the commutative partners and subtraction buddy to go with this problem?

4. _____, _____ and _____ said they didn't have pets, but each drew a picture of the pet they would like to have. _____ said he had pictures of 6 horses he would like to own if he could. What was the total number of animal pictures?

5. _____ collected plastic farm animal babies. He had 9 little piglets and 6 baby calves. How many toy piglets and calves all together?

6. _____'s grandfather had a farm. She loved the baby chicks. There were 6 new fuzzy black chicks and 8 fuzzy yellow chicks. How many fuzzy baby chicks did her grandfather have?

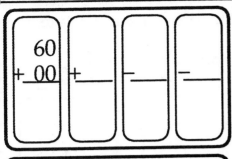

60 FACT FAMILY

"Now we're developing MATH MUSCLE."

Use what you know to find the answer for each printed problem, then write all the problems that belong to the same family.

Circle the regrouping pairs for add and subtract.

Look carefully at the problems.

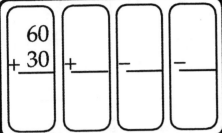
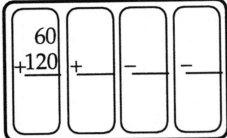
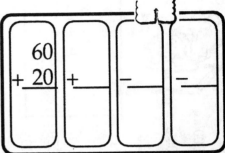

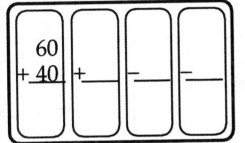
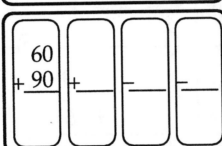
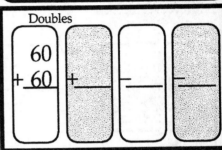

Doubles

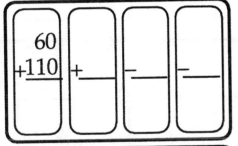
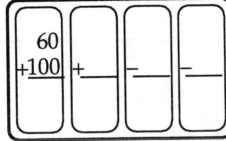
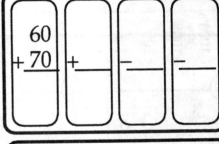

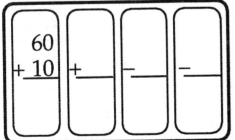
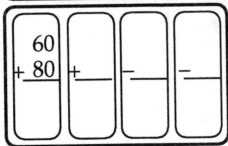
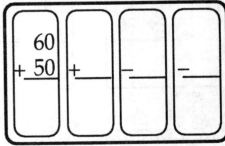

review

60 + 70 = _____	80 + 60 = _____	140 − 60 = _____	180 − 120 = _____
60 + 100 = _____	90 + 60 = _____	100 − 60 = _____	150 − 90 = _____
60 + 80 = _____	70 + 60 = _____	120 − 60 = _____	140 − 80 = _____
60 + 90 = _____	100+ 60 = _____	90 − 60 = _____	160 − 100 = _____
60 + 110 = _____	110+ 60 = _____	110 − 60 = _____	130 − 70 = _____
60 + 120 = _____	120+ 60 = _____	130 − 60 = _____	170 − 110 = _____

Use the Dollar, Dime and Penny Chart to help solve these problems.
Regroup from right to left, then answer the problems from left to right. Soon you will be able to regroup mentally.

♥ ADD

"This is fun when you know what you're doing!!!"

1   100's | 10's | 1's

$$\begin{array}{cc} 2 & 4 \\ + & 6 \\ \hline \end{array}$$

2   100's | 10's | 1's

$$\begin{array}{cc} 3 & 5 \\ + & 6 \\ \hline \end{array}$$

3   100's | 10's | 1's

$$\begin{array}{cc} 7 & 6 \\ + & 6 \\ \hline \end{array}$$

4   100's | 10's | 1's

$$\begin{array}{cc} 2 & 7 \\ + & 6 \\ \hline \end{array}$$

5   100's | 10's | 1's

$$\begin{array}{cc} 4 & 8 \\ + & 6 \\ \hline \end{array}$$

6   1000's | 100's | 10's | 1's

$$\begin{array}{cc} 4 & 4 \\ + & 6 \\ \hline \end{array}$$

7   1000's | 100's | 10's | 1's

$$\begin{array}{cc} 1 & 5 \\ + & 6 \\ \hline \end{array}$$

8   1000's | 100's | 10's | 1's

$$\begin{array}{cc} 2 & 9 \\ + & 6 \\ \hline \end{array}$$

9   1000's | 100's | 10's | 1's

$$\begin{array}{cc} 4 & 7 \\ + & 6 \\ \hline \end{array}$$

10   1000's | 100's | 10's | 1's

$$\begin{array}{cc} 2 & 8 \\ + & 6 \\ \hline \end{array}$$

11   1000's | 100's | 10's | 1's

$$\begin{array}{cc} 3 & 8 \\ + & 6 \\ \hline \end{array}$$

12   1000's | 100's | 10's | 1's

$$\begin{array}{cc} 1 & 9 \\ + & 6 \\ \hline \end{array}$$

13   1000's | 100's | 10's | 1's

$$\begin{array}{cc} 2 & 5 \\ + & 6 \\ \hline \end{array}$$

14   1000's | 100's | 10's | 1's

$$\begin{array}{cc} 3 & 7 \\ + & 6 \\ \hline \end{array}$$

15   1000's | 100's | 10's | 1's

$$\begin{array}{cc} 4 & 8 \\ + & 6 \\ \hline \end{array}$$

16   1000's | 100's | 10's | 1's

$$\begin{array}{ccc} 3 & 4 & 5 \\ + & 6 & 0 \\ \hline \end{array}$$

17   1000's | 100's | 10's | 1's

$$\begin{array}{ccc} 2 & 7 & 9 \\ + & 6 & 0 \\ \hline \end{array}$$

18   1000's | 100's | 10's | 1's

$$\begin{array}{ccc} 5 & 2 & 4 \\ + & 6 & 6 \\ \hline \end{array}$$

19   1000's | 100's | 10's | 1's

$$\begin{array}{ccc} 4 & 2 & 6 \\ + & 6 & 6 \\ \hline \end{array}$$

20   1000's | 100's | 10's | 1's

$$\begin{array}{ccc} 1 & 4 & 9 \\ + & 6 & 0 \\ \hline \end{array}$$

Use the Dollar, Dime and Penny Chart to help solve these problems.
Regroup, then work the problem.

"I've learned
the - 6 facts so
I can do this!"

	10's	1's
1	2	0
	−	6

	10's	1's
2	3	1
	−	6

	1000's	100's	10's	1's
3			4	2
			−	6

	1000's	100's	10's	1's
4			5	3
			−	6

	1000's	100's	10's	1's
5			6	4
			−	6

	1000's	100's	10's	1's
6			7	5
			−	6

	1000's	100's	10's	1's
7			8	0
			−	6

	1000's	100's	10's	1's
8			2	1
			−	6

	1000's	100's	10's	1's
9			3	1
			−	6

	1000's	100's	10's	1's
10			4	2
			−	6

	1000's	100's	10's	1's
11			8	1
			−	6

	1000's	100's	10's	1's
12			5	3
			−	6

	1000's	100's	10's	1's
13			7	4
			−	6

	1000's	100's	10's	1's
14			4	5
		−	6	

	1000's	100's	10's	1's
15			9	2
		−	6	6

	1000's	100's	10's	1's
16			8	5
		−	6	6

	1000's	100's	10's	1's
17			8	4
		−	6	6

	1000's	100's	10's	1's
18			9	2
		−	6	6

	1000's	100's	10's	1's
19			7	1
		−	1	6

	1000's	100's	10's	1's
20		8	9	2
	−	6	6	6

+ 6 RAPID WRITER

A. Write the answers for all of the + 6 facts as fast as you can.

6+1= ___	6+7= ___	6+9= ___
6+5= ___	6+10= ___	6+6= ___
6+3= ___	6+2= ___	6+11= ___
6+4= ___	6+12= ___	6+10= ___
6+7= ___	6+1= ___	6+8= ___
6+2= ___	6+11= ___	6+5= ___
6+9= ___	6+4= ___	6+12= ___
6+6= ___	6+3= ___	6+4= ___
6+12= ___	6+6= ___	6+7= ___
6+10= ___	6+9= ___	6+1= ___
6+8= ___	6+5= ___	6+3= ___
6+11= ___	6+8= ___	6+2= ___

"Keep paddling!

You will soon be sailing through these!"

B. How fast can you write the answers to these number pairs ?

6+5= ___	6+7= ___	6+9= ___
6+8= ___	6+6= ___	6+8= ___
6+6= ___	6+9= ___	6+6= ___
6+4= ___	6+4= ___	6+7= ___
6+9= ___	6+8= ___	6+4= ___
6+7= ___	6+5= ___	6+9= ___
6+8= ___	6+9= ___	6+5= ___
6+9= ___	6+7= ___	6+4= ___
6+6= ___	6+5= ___	6+7= ___
6+5= ___	6+8= ___	6+6= ___
6+4= ___	6+4= ___	6+5= ___
6+7= ___	6+6= ___	6+8= ___

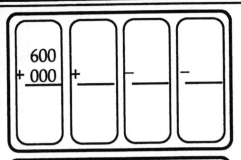

600 FACT FAMILY

Use what you know to find the answer for each printed problem, then write all the problems that belong to the same family.

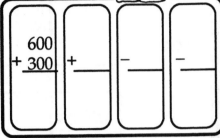

Circle the regrouping pairs for add and subtract.

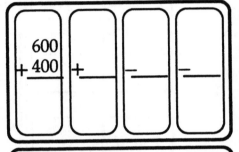

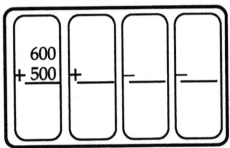

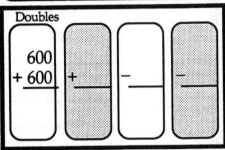

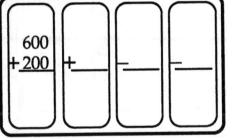

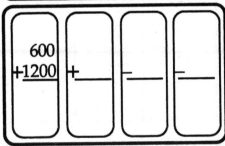

Doubles

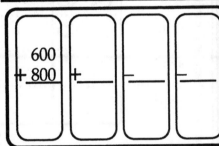

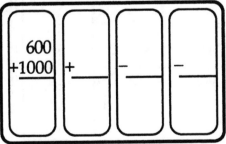

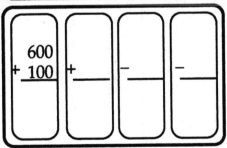

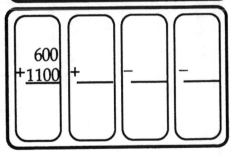

review

600 + 700 =_____	800 + 600=_____	1400 − 600 =_____	1800 − 1200 =_____
600 + 1000 =_____	900 + 600=_____	1000 − 600 =_____	1500 − 900 =_____
600 + 800 =_____	700 + 600=_____	1200 − 600 =_____	1400 − 800 =_____
600 + 900 =_____	1000 + 600=_____	900 − 600 =_____	1600 − 1000 =_____
600 + 1100 =_____	1100 + 600=_____	1100 − 600 =_____	1300 − 700 =_____
600 + 1200 =_____	1200 + 600=_____	1300 − 600=_____	1700 − 1100 =_____

POWER PAGE

WATCH THE SIGNS! Use your Dollar, Dimes and Pennies Chart if you need to.

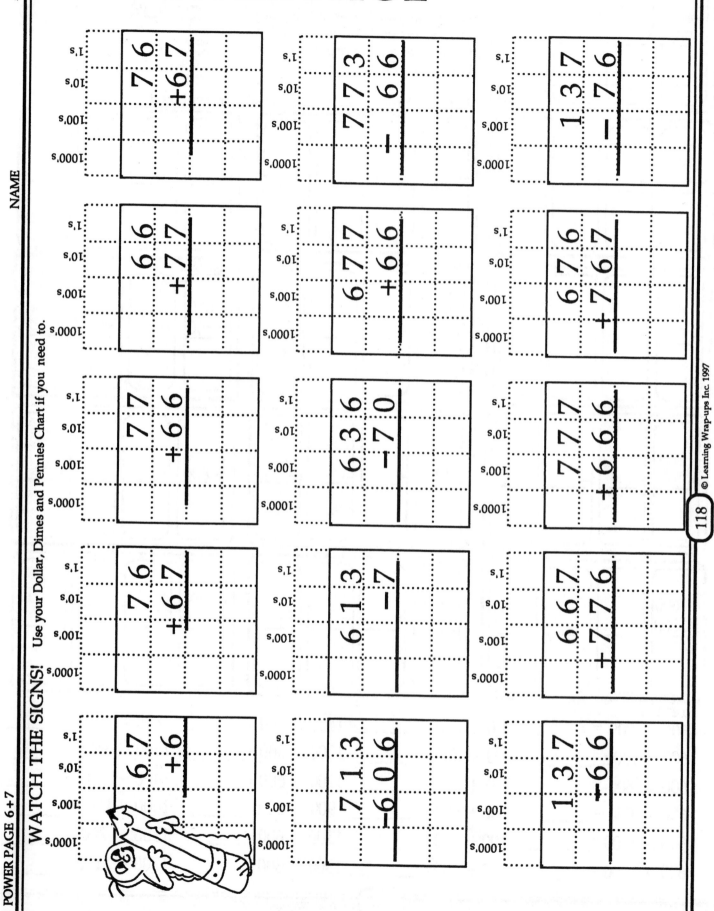

$$76 + 67$$

$$773 - 66$$

$$137 - 76$$

$$66 + 77$$

$$677 + 66$$

$$676 + 767$$

$$77 + 66$$

$$636 - 70$$

$$777 + 666$$

$$76 + 67$$

$$613 - 7$$

$$667 + 776$$

$$67 + 6$$

$$713 - 606$$

$$137 + 66$$

Watch the signs!

+ - 6 THINKER SHEET

10 +6 = 16	7 -6 = 1	15 -9 = 6	6 +6 = 12	1 +6 = 7	16 -6 = 10	11 -5 = 6	6 -5 = 1
6 +2 = 8	4 +6 = 10	17 -11 = 6	7 +6 = 13	13 -7 = 6	9 +6 = 15	18 -6 = 12	6 -3 = 3
14 -6 = 8	6 +0 = 6	6 +12 = 18	9 -6 = 3	6 +7 = 13	12 +6 = 18	6 +6 = 12	6 -1 = 5
18 -12 = 6	13 -6 = 7	6 +8 = 14	6 +5 = 11	12 -6 = 6	8 -2 = 6	6 +10 = 16	6 -2 = 4
70 -10 = 60	150 -60 = 90	60 -10 = 50	110 -60 = 50	90 -30 = 60	50 +60 = 110	60 -10 = 50	60 -40 = 20
60 -10 = 50	60 +30 = 90	60 -60 = 0	60 +90 = 150	80 +60 = 140	80 -60 = 20	120 -60 = 60	110 -60 = 50

Say: 6 hundred add 11 hundred.

Say: 17 hundred subtract 6 hundred.

Say: 10 hundred subtract 4 hundred.

600 +600 = 1200	100 -60 = 40	140 -80 = 60	600 +1100 = 1700	300 +600 = 900	1700 -600 = 1100	600 +400 = 1000	1000 -400 = 600

Say: 12 hundred.

Say: 17 hundred.

Say: 11 hundred

LESSON PLANS FOR TEACHING + - 7

1. Look at the HERE'S WHAT I KNOW Chart. Count the number of + - 7 problems that still need to be learned. Have students list all the problems they have already learned. There is only 7 + 8, 7 + 9, their COMMUTATIVE PARTNERS and the SUBTRACTION BUDDIES left to learn. Ask them if there is any way they can figure out the answers for these two problems. Have them tell you how they did it.

2. Do the PENNY PAGES for + and - 7, pp. 121, 122. Use manipulatives with the students who still need to use them. Use the **Learning Wrap-ups** as directed on the worksheets. Remind students that you expect them to write all the answers quickly, because they know the Commutative Partners and Subtraction Buddies. Be sure to drill with the Wrap-ups as indicated on the sheets.

3. Have students do the 7 COMMUTATIVE PARTNERS and SUBTRACTION BUDDIES, p 123.

4. Do the + - 7 FACT FAMILY worksheet, p. 124.

5. Do + 7 WORD PROBLEMS, p. 125.

6. Work through the + and - 7 REGROUPING worksheets, pp. 127, 128. If students are having any problems with regrouping, be sure to have them get out their DDP charts.

7. Do the + - 70 FACT FAMILY, p. 126.

8. Do the + - 700 FACT FAMILY, p. 129.

9. Do POWER PAGE with 7, 8 and 5, p. 130. You may want to do more problems. Use the STUDENT POWER PAGE, p. 30, to write them on. Better - give the students the blank page and ask them to write some problems. You will know if they understand the regrouping concept when they do this.

10. Pair up students to do the + - 7 THINKER SHEET, p. 131.

11. SEND HOME the + and - 7 LEARNING WRAP-UPS and the + 7 RAPID WRITER SHEET, p. 132. Tell students to ask someone to time how fast they can write one column. Do the Wrap-up 5 times, then write another column. Repeat the process until all the columns have been done.

NEXT DAY

- Have a WRAP-OFF with the + and - 6, + and - 7 **Wrap-ups.**
- Give the + - 7 QUICK QUIZ.
- Color the HERE'S WHAT I KNOW Chart.

© Learning Wrap-ups Inc. 1997

COVER THE CIRCLES WITH PENNIES OR DISCS TO COMPLETE THESE PROBLEMS.

+7 PENNY PAGE

Always start at 1 when covering the number circles to help solve problems.

1	2	3	4	5	6	7	8	9	**10**
11	12	13	14	15	16	17	18	19	**20**

(circles numbered 1–20, with 10 and 20 shaded)

A.

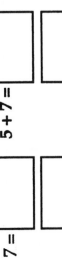

"Have a friend or parent give you a quiz on the problems with regrouping pairs in the darker print. Tell them the answers as fast as you can."

Use pennies or discs to solve these problems.

1 + 7 = ☐

5 + 7 = ☐

9 + 7 = ☐

2 + 7 = ☐

6 + 7 = ☐

10 + 7 = ☐

3 + 7 = ☐

7 + 7 = ☐

11 + 7 = ☐

4 + 7 = ☐

8 + 7 = ☐

12 + 7 = ☐

Each student should have 20 pennies and a dime. Make certain all the problems in section A are correct. Exchange 10 pennies for a dime when appropriate.

Use the #7 Addition Learning Wrap-up, and do it at least 10 times. Be sure to say the problems and answers aloud.

Remind students of the commutative properties of addition, before they do the set of problems. They then fold papers in half and do the problems in section B.

Do the #7 Addition Learning Wrap-up and mark a square each time you do it correctly.

☐☐ ☐☐ ☐ ☐ ☐ ☐ ☐ ☒

Can you do these problems without covering the circles?

B.

1 + 7	2 + 7	3 + 7	4 + 7	5 + 7	6 + 7
7 + 7	8 + 7	9 + 7	10 + 7	11 + 7	12 + 7
7 + 1	7 + 4	7 + 10	7 + 7	7 + 8	7 + 5
7 + 12	7 + 2	7 + 3	7 + 6	7 + 9	7 + 11

- 7 PENNY PAGE

Always start at 1 when covering the number circles to solve problems.
To take away or subtract, remove discs or pennies starting from the last circle you covered.

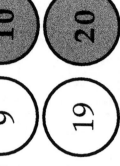

(1) (2) (3) (4) (5) (6) (7) (8) (9) **(10)**

(11) (12) (13) (14) (15) (16) (17) (18) (19) **(20)**

A.

Use pennies or discs to solve these problems.

7 - 7 = ☐	12 - 7 = ☐	17 - 7 = ☐
8 - 7 = ☐	13 - 7 = ☐	18 - 7 = ☐
9 - 7 = ☐	14 - 7 = ☐	19 - 7 = ☐
10 - 7 = ☐	15 - 7 = ☐	20 - 7 = ☐
11 - 7 = ☐	16 - 7 = ☐	

B.

Do the #7 Subtraction Learning Wrap-up and mark a square each time you do it correctly.

☐ ☐ ☐ ☐ ☐ ☐ ☐ ☐
☒ ☐ ☐ ☐ ☐ ☐ ☐ ☐

Can you do these problems without using pennies or discs?

$\begin{array}{r}7\\-7\end{array}$	$\begin{array}{r}8\\-7\end{array}$	$\begin{array}{r}9\\-7\end{array}$	$\begin{array}{r}10\\-7\end{array}$	$\begin{array}{r}11\\-7\end{array}$	$\begin{array}{r}12\\-7\end{array}$
$\begin{array}{r}13\\-7\end{array}$	$\begin{array}{r}14\\-7\end{array}$	$\begin{array}{r}15\\-7\end{array}$	$\begin{array}{r}16\\-7\end{array}$	$\begin{array}{r}17\\-7\end{array}$	$\begin{array}{r}18\\-7\end{array}$
$\begin{array}{r}17\\-7\end{array}$	$\begin{array}{r}14\\-7\end{array}$	$\begin{array}{r}13\\-7\end{array}$	$\begin{array}{r}15\\-7\end{array}$	$\begin{array}{r}19\\-7\end{array}$	$\begin{array}{r}12\\-7\end{array}$
$\begin{array}{r}16\\-7\end{array}$	$\begin{array}{r}10\\-7\end{array}$	$\begin{array}{r}18\\-7\end{array}$	$\begin{array}{r}8\\-7\end{array}$	$\begin{array}{r}11\\-7\end{array}$	$\begin{array}{r}9\\-7\end{array}$

"Remember: what you know about addition helps you solve subtraction problems."

Each student should have 20 pennies and a dime. Be certain students have all the answers in section A correct. Emphasize that any number subtracted from itself equals 0.

Do #7 Subtract Learning Wrap-up, saying problems and answers aloud ten times. Then fold the paper and do section B for more practice.

COMMUTATIVE PARTNERS   SUBTRACTION BUDDIES

$1+7=$ ___	$7+1=$ ___	$8-7=$ ___	$8-1=$ ___
$2+7=$ ___	$7+2=$ ___	$9-7=$ ___	$9-2=$ ___
$3+7=$ ___	$7+3=$ ___	$10-7=$ ___	$10-3=$ ___
$4+7=$ ___	$7+4=$ ___	$11-7=$ ___	$11-4=$ ___
$5+7=$ ___	$7+5=$ ___	$12-7=$ ___	$12-5=$ ___
$6+7=$ ___	$7+6=$ ___	$13-7=$ ___	$13-6=$ ___
$7+7=$ ___	$7+7=$ ___	$14-7=$ ___	$14-7=$ ___
$8+3=$ ___	$7+8=$ ___	$15-7=$ ___	$15-8=$ ___
$9+3=$ ___	$7+9=$ ___	$16-7=$ ___	$16-9=$ ___
$10+3=$ ___	$7+10=$ ___	$17-7=$ ___	$17-10=$ ___
$11+3=$ ___	$7+11=$ ___	$18-7=$ ___	$18-11=$ ___
$12+3=$ ___	$7+12=$ ___	$19-7=$ ___	$19-12=$ ___

7 FACT FAMILY

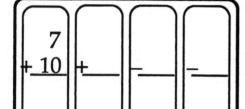

Use what you know to find the answer for each printed problem, then write all the problems that belong to the same family.

"This is not that tough! I knew lots of answers before I even started"

Circle the numbers that need to be regrouped.

$\begin{array}{r} 7 \\ + 10 \\ \hline \end{array}$ +___ −___ −___

$\begin{array}{r} 7 \\ + 9 \\ \hline \end{array}$ +___ −___ −___

$\begin{array}{r} 7 \\ + 3 \\ \hline \end{array}$ +___ −___ −___

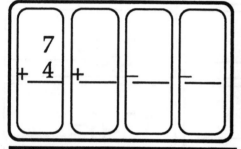

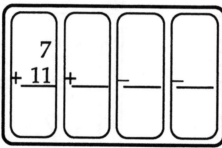

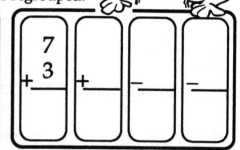

$\begin{array}{r} 7 \\ + 4 \\ \hline \end{array}$ +___ −___ −___

$\begin{array}{r} 7 \\ + 11 \\ \hline \end{array}$ +___ −___ −___

$\begin{array}{r} 7 \\ + 6 \\ \hline \end{array}$ +___ −___ −___

Doubles

$\begin{array}{r} 7 \\ + 7 \\ \hline \end{array}$ +___ −___ −___

$\begin{array}{r} 7 \\ + 12 \\ \hline \end{array}$ +___ −___ −___

$\begin{array}{r} 7 \\ + 1 \\ \hline \end{array}$ +___ −___ −___

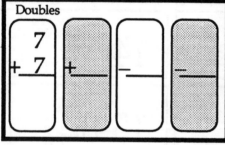

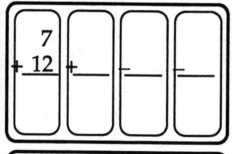

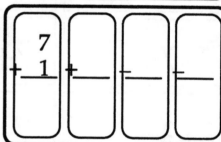

$\begin{array}{r} 7 \\ + 2 \\ \hline \end{array}$ +___ −___ −___

$\begin{array}{r} 7 \\ + 8 \\ \hline \end{array}$ +___ −___ −___

$\begin{array}{r} 7 \\ + 5 \\ \hline \end{array}$ +___ −___ −___

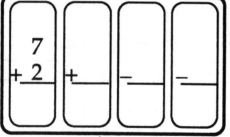

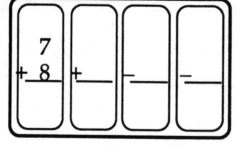

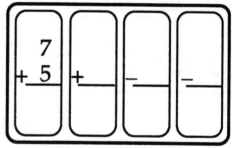

review

7 + 7 =____	8 + 7 =____	14 − 7 =____	19 − 12 =____
7 + 10 =____	9 + 7 =____	10 − 7 =____	16 − 9 =____
7 + 8 =____	7 + 7 =____	12 − 7 =____	15 − 8 =____
7 + 9 =____	10 + 7 =____	9 − 7 =____	17 − 10 =____
7 + 11 =____	11 + 7 =____	11 − 7 =____	14 − 7 =____
7 + 12 =____	12 + 7 =____	13 − 7 =____	18 − 11 =____

HELPING IN THE LIBRARY

Our class helped put new books in the library.   These are the problems we wrote about our experience. We also can write COMMUTATIVE PARTNERS and SUBTRACTION BUDDIES for each of the story problem facts.

1. _____carried 7 books from the storage room to the library. _____ carried 9 more. How many books did the two of them carry?

     _____ _____

     _____ _____

2. _____ put 8 books about animals on the shelf. _____put away 7 books about magic tricks. What was the total number of books they put away?

     _____ _____

     _____ _____

3. _____glued checkout envelopes in the front of 7 books. _____ glued in 6 envelopes. How many books did they glue envelopes in?

     _____ _____

     _____ _____

4. _____counted 7 books about rockets. _____ brought 7 more rocket books from the storage room. How many books were there about rockets?

     _____ _____

     _____ _____

5. The librarian, _____, asked _____to count the number of boxes we had emptied. There were 12. _____ counted the full boxes in the storage room. There were 7. How many boxes of books were there all together?

     _____ _____

     _____ _____

6. When we were through helping, _____ said there were 5 books she wanted to check out. _____ and _____ checked out 7 more. How many books did the three of them check out?

     _____ _____

     _____ _____

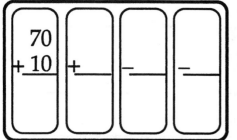

70 FACT FAMILY

"It doesn't take a superman to do these!"

Use what you know to find the answer for each printed problem, then write all the problems that belong to the same family.

Watch the order of the problems!

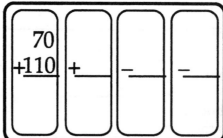

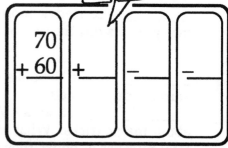

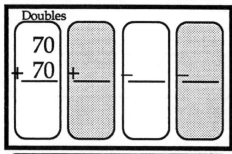

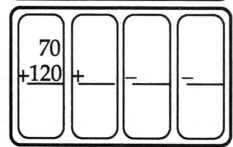

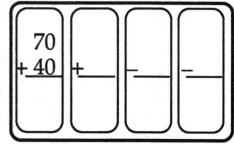

Doubles

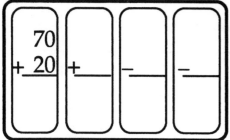

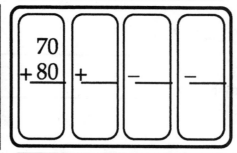

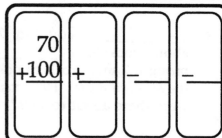

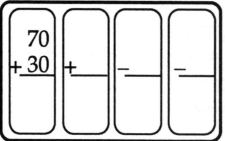

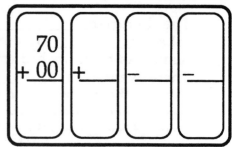

review

70 + 70 = ___	80 + 70 = ___	140 − 70 = ___	160 − 90 = ___
70 + 40 = ___	90 + 70 = ___	100 − 70 = ___	110 − 40 = ___
70 + 80 = ___	70 + 70 = ___	120 − 70 = ___	140 − 70 = ___
70 + 90 = ___	40 + 70 = ___	90 − 70 = ___	150 − 80 = ___
70 + 50 = ___	50 + 70 = ___	110 − 70 = ___	120 − 50 = ___
70 + 70 = ___	70 + 70 = ___	130 − 70 = ___	100 − 30 = ___

ADD

Use your Dollar, Dime and Penny Chart if you need to.

"Just checking to see if you know what to do."

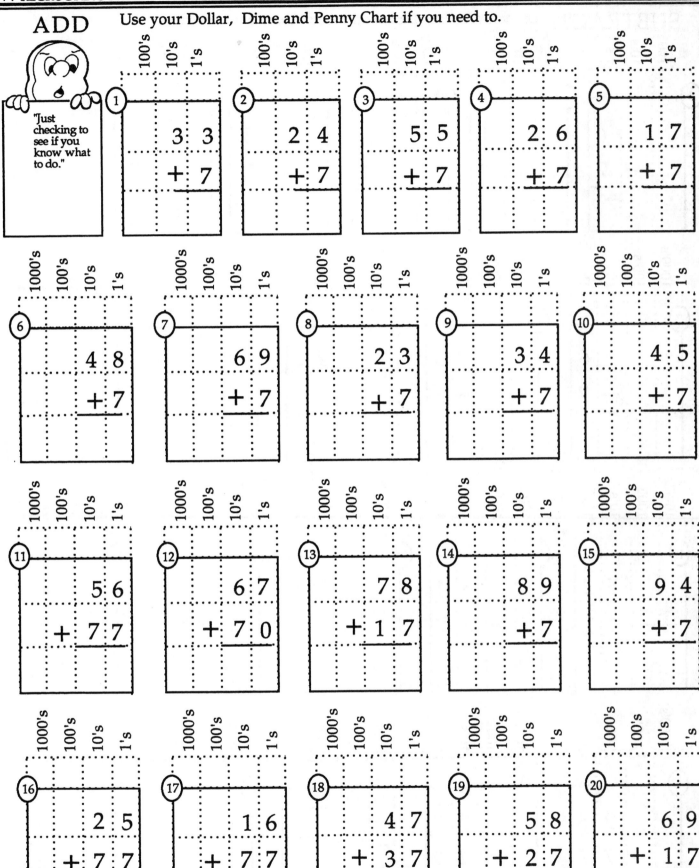

1.
$$\begin{array}{r} 3\ 3 \\ +\ 7 \\ \hline \end{array}$$

2.
$$\begin{array}{r} 2\ 4 \\ +\ 7 \\ \hline \end{array}$$

3.
$$\begin{array}{r} 5\ 5 \\ +\ 7 \\ \hline \end{array}$$

4.
$$\begin{array}{r} 2\ 6 \\ +\ 7 \\ \hline \end{array}$$

5.
$$\begin{array}{r} 1\ 7 \\ +\ 7 \\ \hline \end{array}$$

6.
$$\begin{array}{r} 4\ 8 \\ +\ 7 \\ \hline \end{array}$$

7.
$$\begin{array}{r} 6\ 9 \\ +\ 7 \\ \hline \end{array}$$

8.
$$\begin{array}{r} 2\ 3 \\ +\ 7 \\ \hline \end{array}$$

9.
$$\begin{array}{r} 3\ 4 \\ +\ 7 \\ \hline \end{array}$$

10.
$$\begin{array}{r} 4\ 5 \\ +\ 7 \\ \hline \end{array}$$

11.
$$\begin{array}{r} 5\ 6 \\ +\ 7\ 7 \\ \hline \end{array}$$

12.
$$\begin{array}{r} 6\ 7 \\ +\ 7\ 0 \\ \hline \end{array}$$

13.
$$\begin{array}{r} 7\ 8 \\ +\ 1\ 7 \\ \hline \end{array}$$

14.
$$\begin{array}{r} 8\ 9 \\ +\ 7 \\ \hline \end{array}$$

15.
$$\begin{array}{r} 9\ 4 \\ +\ 7 \\ \hline \end{array}$$

16.
$$\begin{array}{r} 2\ 5 \\ +\ 7\ 7 \\ \hline \end{array}$$

17.
$$\begin{array}{r} 1\ 6 \\ +\ 7\ 7 \\ \hline \end{array}$$

18.
$$\begin{array}{r} 4\ 7 \\ +\ 3\ 7 \\ \hline \end{array}$$

19.
$$\begin{array}{r} 5\ 8 \\ +\ 2\ 7 \\ \hline \end{array}$$

20.
$$\begin{array}{r} 6\ 9 \\ +\ 1\ 7 \\ \hline \end{array}$$

SUBTRACT   Use your Dollar, Dime and Penny Chart if you need to.

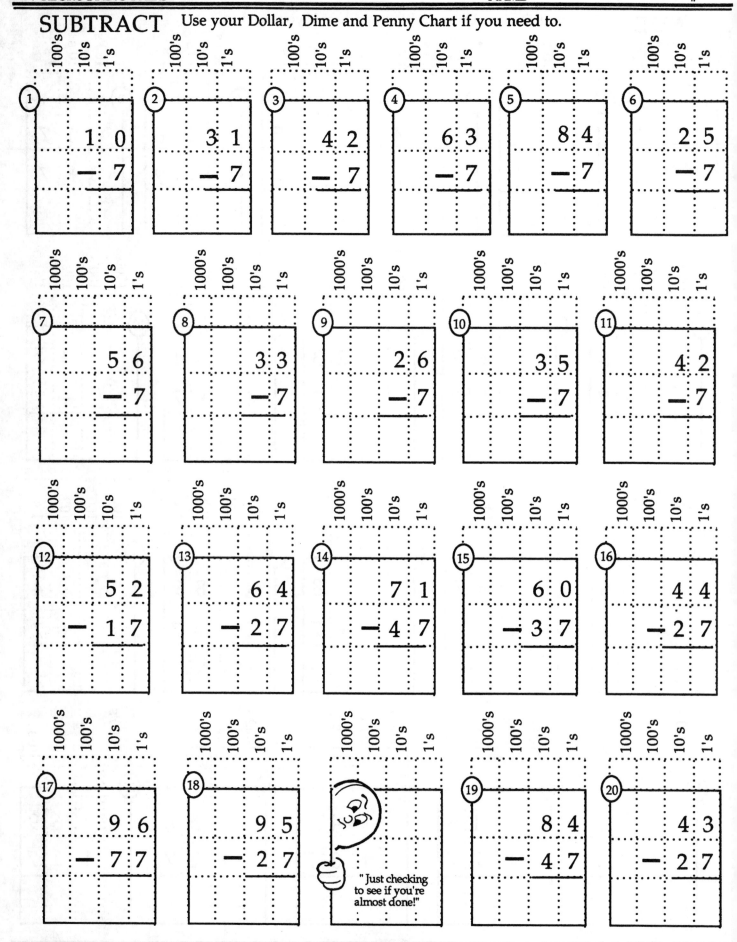

1. (100's / 10's / 1's)
```
  1 0
-   7
```

2. (100's / 10's / 1's)
```
  3 1
-   7
```

3. (100's / 10's / 1's)
```
  4 2
-   7
```

4. (100's / 10's / 1's)
```
  6 3
-   7
```

5. (100's / 10's / 1's)
```
  8 4
-   7
```

6. (100's / 10's / 1's)
```
  2 5
-   7
```

7. (1000's / 100's / 10's / 1's)
```
  5 6
-   7
```

8. (1000's / 100's / 10's / 1's)
```
  3 3
-   7
```

9. (1000's / 100's / 10's / 1's)
```
  2 6
-   7
```

10. (1000's / 100's / 10's / 1's)
```
  3 5
-   7
```

11. (1000's / 100's / 10's / 1's)
```
  4 2
-   7
```

12. (1000's / 100's / 10's / 1's)
```
  5 2
- 1 7
```

13. (1000's / 100's / 10's / 1's)
```
  6 4
- 2 7
```

14. (1000's / 100's / 10's / 1's)
```
  7 1
- 4 7
```

15. (1000's / 100's / 10's / 1's)
```
  6 0
- 3 7
```

16. (1000's / 100's / 10's / 1's)
```
  4 4
- 2 7
```

17. (1000's / 100's / 10's / 1's)
```
  9 6
- 7 7
```

18. (1000's / 100's / 10's / 1's)
```
  9 5
- 2 7
```

" Just checking to see if you're almost done!"

19. (1000's / 100's / 10's / 1's)
```
  8 4
- 4 7
```

20. (1000's / 100's / 10's / 1's)
```
  4 3
- 2 7
```

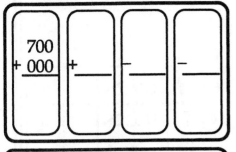

700 FACT FAMILY

Use what you know to find the answer for each printed problem, then write all the problems that belong to the same family.

Check the order of the problems.

"Give yourself a big cheer when you finish this page!"

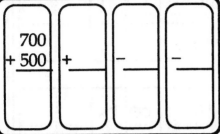
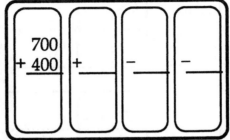
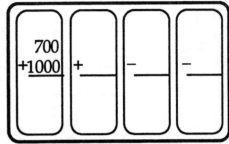

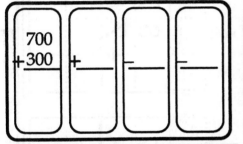
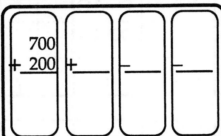
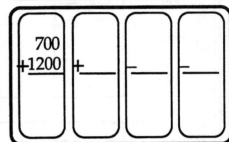

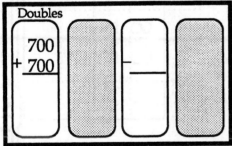
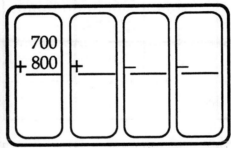
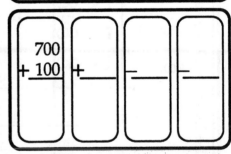

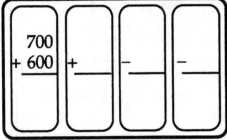
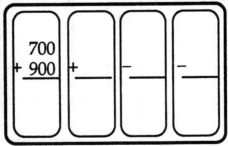
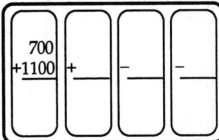

review

700 + 700 =	800 + 700 =	1400 − 700 =	1800 − 1100 =
700 + 1000 =	900 + 700 =	1000 − 700 =	1500 − 800 =
700 + 800 =	700 + 700 =	1200 − 700 =	1400 − 700 =
700 + 900 =	1000 + 700 =	900 − 700 =	1600 − 900 =
700 + 1100 =	1100 + 700 =	1100 − 700 =	1300 − 600 =
700 + 1200 =	1200 + 700 =	1300 − 700 =	1700 − 1000 =

POWER PAGE 7+8

WATCH THE SIGNS!   Use the Dollars, Dimes and Pennies Chart if you need help.

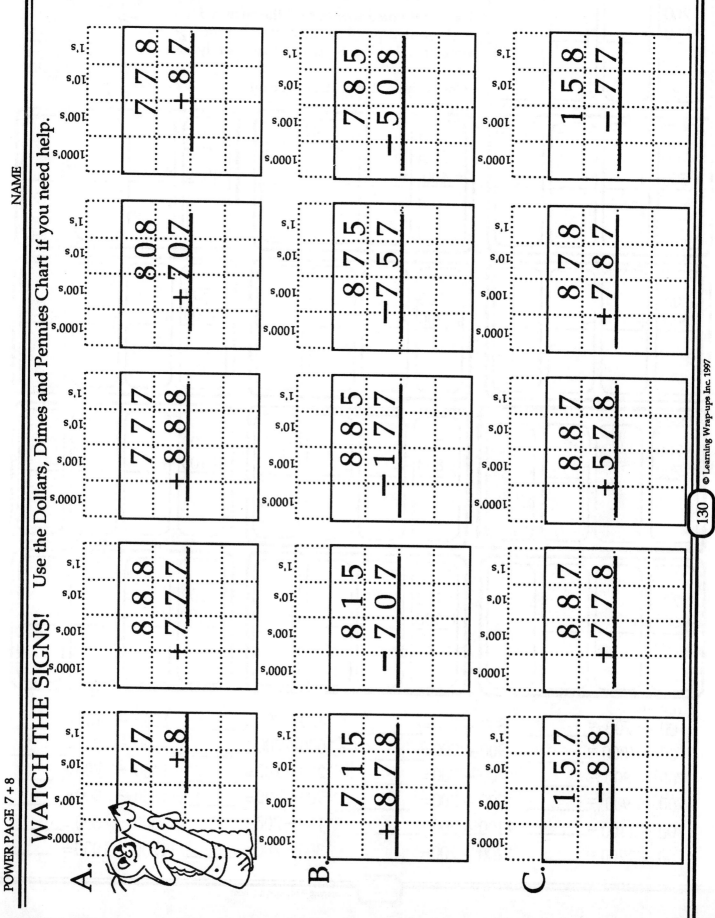

A.

```
   7 7 8
 +   8 7
---------
```

```
   8 0 8
 + 7 0 7
---------
```

```
   7 7 7
 + 8 8 8
---------
```

```
   8 8 8
 + 7 7 7
---------
```

```
     7 7
 +     8
---------
```

B.

```
   7 8 5
 - 5 0 8
---------
```

```
   8 7 5
 - 7 5 7
---------
```

```
   8 8 5
 - 1 7 7
---------
```

```
   8 1 5
 - 7 0 7
---------
```

```
   7 1 5
 + 8 7 8
---------
```

C.

```
   1 5 8
 -   7 7
---------
```

```
   8 7 8
 + 7 8 7
---------
```

```
   8 8 7
 + 5 7 8
---------
```

```
   8 8 7
 + 7 7 8
---------
```

```
   1 5 7
 -   8 8
---------
```

130

+ - 7 THINKER SHEET

Two students work together. One reads the problems, the other gives the answers from memory. Take turns reading the problems.

Watch the signs!

7 -1 ___ 6	18 -7 ___ 11	15 -8 ___ 7	7 +6 ___ 13	5 +7 ___ 12	17 -7 ___ 10	10 -3 ___ 7	7 -6 ___ 1
7 +9 ___ 16	7 +7 ___ 14	13 -7 ___ 6	8 -1 ___ 7	7 +3 ___ 10	12 +7 ___ 19	11 -7 ___ 4	7 -2 ___ 5
7 +5 ___ 12	3 +7 ___ 10	12 -7 ___ 5	17 -10 ___ 7	7 +10 ___ 17	4 +7 ___ 11	14 -7 ___ 7	7 -4 ___ 3
11 -4 ___ 7	7 +7 ___ 14	6 +7 ___ 13	9 -7 ___ 2	14 -7 ___ 7	7 +11 ___ 18	10 +7 ___ 17	7 -5 ___ 2
90 -20 ___ 70	160 -90 ___ 70	70 +10 ___ 80	80 +70 ___ 150	190 -70 ___ 120	120 -50 ___ 70	70 +40 ___ 110	70 -30 ___ 40
110 +70 ___ 180	190 -120 ___ 70	70 +10 ___ 80	70 +120 ___ 190	100 -70 ___ 30	160 -70 ___ 90	70 -20 ___ 50	70 -70 ___ 0

Say:
18 hundred
subtract
11 hundred.

	Say: 15 hundred.	Say: 13 hundred.					
300 +700 ___ 1000	1500 -700 ___ 800	1300 -600 ___ 700	700 +800 ___ 1500	900 +700 ___ 1600	800 -700 ___ 100	1800 -1100 ___ 700	700 +200 ___ 900

Say: 10 hundred,
or 1 thousand.

Say:15
hundred.

Say: 16
hundred.

+ 7 RAPID WRITER

NAME _____ #

A. Write the answers to one column of facts as fast as you can. Then wrap a Wrap-up 5 times. Repeat with all three columns.

"Wrap-up, Write, Wrap-up, Write! Learn to add 7, In just one night."

$7+1=$	$7+10=$	$7+7=$
$7+5=$	$7+9=$	$7+4=$
$7+3=$	$7+1=$	$7+11=$
$7+4=$	$7+7=$	$7+8=$
$7+7=$	$7+11=$	$7+6=$
$7+2=$	$7+4=$	$7+1=$
$7+9=$	$7+6=$	$7+9=$
$7+6=$	$7+5=$	$7+12=$
$7+12=$	$7+2=$	$7+5=$
$7+10=$	$7+8=$	$7+3=$
$7+8=$	$7+3=$	$7+2=$
$7+11=$	$7+12=$	$7+10=$

B. How fast can you write the answers for these regrouping pairs?

$7+3=$	$7+3=$	$7+7=$
$7+7=$	$7+5=$	$7+8=$
$7+8=$	$7+9=$	$7+3=$
$7+5=$	$7+7=$	$7+9=$
$7+4=$	$7+4=$	$7+5=$
$7+9=$	$7+8=$	$7+6=$
$7+6=$	$7+6=$	$7+4=$
$7+8=$	$7+3=$	$7+8=$
$7+7=$	$7+4=$	$7+7=$
$7+9=$	$7+8=$	$7+3=$
$7+6=$	$7+6=$	$7+9=$
$7+4=$	$7+7=$	$7+8=$
$7+5=$	$7+9=$	$7+5=$
$7+3=$	$7+5=$	$7+6=$

132

LESSON PLANS FOR TEACHING + - 8

1. Have an ADDITION WRAP-OFF with the + 4, 5, 6, and 7 WRAP-UPS.   Then have a subtract WRAP-OFF with the - 4, 5, 6, and 7 WRAP-UPS. Allow more time to do the subtract WRAP-OFF.

2. TALK ABOUT how many facts are left to learn. Remind students that if they remember that 8 + 8 is 16 from the doubles lesson, they know all but one of the Add 8 facts. Amazing! What fact is left? (8+9, its commutative partner and inverse operations.)

3. Do the + - 8 PENNY PAGES, pp. 134, 135. Use the pennies if necessary. Be sure to fill in the squares as students do the Wrap-ups to go with each page. Continue to encourage and praise the students for what they have accomplished.

4. Do the COMMUTATIVE PARTNERS and SUBTRACTION BUDDIES worksheets, p. 136.

5. Listen to the + 8 and - 8 WRAP-UP RAP tapes. Have students do the WRAP-UP while listening to the tape. Have them call out the answers as they go.

6. Complete the + - 8 FACT FAMILY worksheet, p. 137.

7. Read the + 8 WORD PROBLEMS, to the students, p. 138. Have the students write in the names of their friends and classmates.

8. Work through the + - worksheets for REGROUPING, pp. 140, 141. Have students use their DOLLAR, DIME and PENNY Chart if they are still having problems with place value and regrouping.

9. Do the + 80 FACT FAMILY worksheet, p. 139.

10. Practice doing the - 8 LEARNING WRAP-UP. Do it at least 20 times during the day. Since students have learned all but one of the answers by now, they should be able to do it fairly fast. Alternate the WRAP-UP practice with the PRACTICE THINKING 8's worksheet, p. 142. (Print 2 copies for each student.)

11. Do the + - 800 FACT FAMILY worksheet, p. 143.

12. Have students do the POWER PAGE with the numbers 8 and 9. Write more problems for them on the Students' Blank POWER PAGE, p. 144, if needed.

13. Pair up students to do the + - 8 THINKER SHEET, p. 145.

14. Send home the #8 add and subtract LEARNING WRAP-UPS, along with the PRACTICE THINKING 8's worksheet.

NEXT DAY

- PRACTICE the + 8 and - 8 WRAP-UPS several times.

- Give the + - 8 QUICK QUIZ. p. 24.

- Fill in the HERE'S WHAT I KNOW Chart.

COVER THE CIRCLES WITH PENNIES OR DISCS TO COMPLETE THESE PROBLEMS.

NAME _____ #_____

+ 8 PENNY PAGE

Always start at 1 when covering the number circles to help solve problems.

| 1 | 2 | 3 | 4 | 5 | 6 | 7 | 8 | 9 | 10 |
| 11 | 12 | 13 | 14 | 15 | 16 | 17 | 18 | 19 | 20 |

"It's a bright idea to picture the problems in your mind and say the answers. It will help you memorize the facts quicker."

A. Use pennies or discs to solve these problems.

1 + 8 =

2 + 8 =

3 + 8 =

4 + 8 =

5 + 8 =

6 + 8 =

7 + 8 =

8 + 8 =

9 + 8 =

10 + 8 =

11 + 8 =

12 + 8 =

Each student should have 20 pennies. Make certain all the problems in section A are correct. Trade 10 pennies for a dime when appropriate.

Use the #8 Addition Learning Wrap-up, and do it 12 times. Be sure to say the problems and answers aloud.

Remind students of the commutative properties of addition, before they do set B problems. Have them fold papers in half and do the problems in section B.

Do the #8 Addition Learning Wrap-up and mark a square each time you do it correctly.

☐ ☐ ☐ ☐ ☐
☒ ☐ ☐ ☐ ☐

B. Can you do these problems without covering the circles?

1 + 8	2 + 8	3 + 8	4 + 8	5 + 8	6 + 8
7 + 8	8 + 8	9 + 8	10 + 8	11 + 8	12 + 8
8 + 1	8 + 4	8 + 10	8 + 7	8 + 8	8 + 5
8 + 12	8 + 2	8 + 3	8 + 6	8 + 9	8 + 11

- 8 PENNY PAGE

Always start at 1 when covering the number circles to solve problems.
To take away or subtract, remove discs or pennies starting from the last circle you covered.

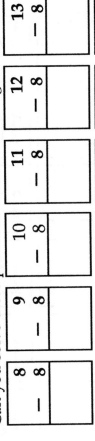

(1) (2) (3) (4) (5) (6) (7) (8) (9) **(10)**

(11) (12) (13) (14) (15) (16) (17) (18) (19) **(20)**

Do the #8 Subtraction Learning Wrap-up and mark a square each time you do it correctly.

☐ ☐ ☐ ☐ ☐ ☐ ☐ ☐ ☐ ☐ ☒

B.

Can you solve these problems without covering the circles?

13 − 8	12 − 8	11 − 8	10 − 8	9 − 8	8 − 8
19 − 8	18 − 8	17 − 8	16 − 8	15 − 8	14 − 8
12 − 8	19 − 8	15 − 8	13 − 8	14 − 8	17 − 8
9 − 8	11 − 8	20 − 8	18 − 8	10 − 8	16 − 8

A.

Use pennies or discs to solve these problems.

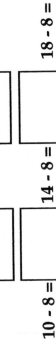

"Now let me think... Can I use what I know about addition to find the answers to these problems?"

8 - 8 =

9 - 8 =

13 - 8 =

17 - 8 =

10 - 8 =

14 - 8 =

18 - 8 =

11 - 8 =

15 - 8 =

19 - 8 =

12 - 8 =

16 - 8 =

20 - 8 =

Each student should have 20 pennies. Be certain students have all the answers in section A correct. Emphasize that any number subtracted from itself equals 0.

Do #8 Subtract Learning Wrap-up, saying problems and answers aloud several times then do section B for more practice.

135

COMMUTATIVE PARTNERS		SUBTRACTION BUDDIES	
1+8= ____	8+1=____	9-8= ____	9-1=____
2+8= ____	8+2=____	10-8= ____	10-2=____
3+8= ____	8+3=____	11-8= ____	11-3=____
4+8= ____	8+4=____	12-8= ____	12-4=____
5+8= ____	8+5=____	13-8= ____	13-5=____
6+8= ____	8+6=____	14-8= ____	14-6=____
7+8= ____	8+7=____	15-8= ____	15-7=____
8+8= ____	8+8=____	16-8= ____	16-8=____
9+8= ____	8+9=____	17-8= ____	17-9=____
10+8= ____	8+10=____	18-8= ____	18-10=____
11+8= ____	8+11=____	19-8= ____	19-11=____
12+8= ____	8+12=____	20-8= ____	20-12=____

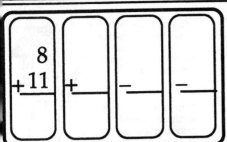

8 FACT FAMILY

Use what you know to find the answer for each printed problem, then write all the problems that belong to the same family.

Circle the number pairs that need regrouping.

"I'm taking giant steps in math by learning the add and subtract facts so well!"

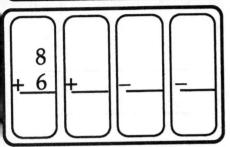

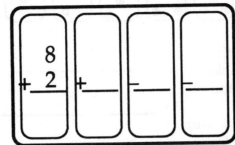

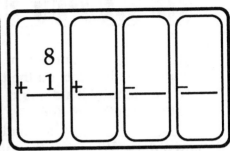

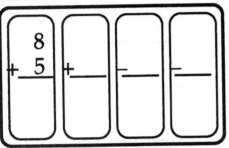

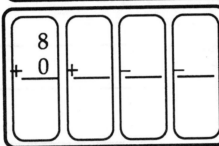

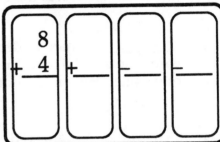

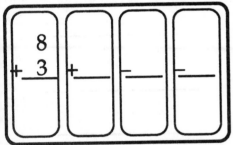

Doubles

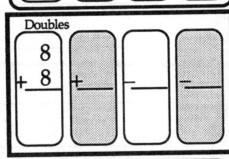

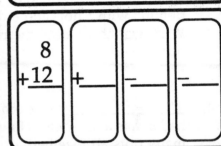

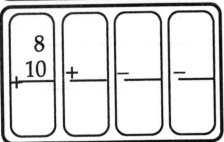

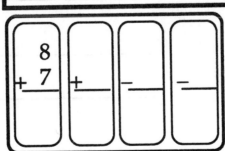

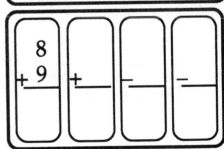

review

8 + 7 =_____	8 + 8 =_____	14 − 8 = _____	20 − 12 = _____
8 + 10 =_____	9 + 8 =_____	10 − 8 = _____	17 − 9 = _____
8 + 8 =_____	7 + 8 =_____	12 − 8 = _____	16 − 8 = _____
8 + 9 =_____	10 + 8 =_____	9 − 8 = _____	18 − 10 = _____
8 + 11 =_____	11 + 8 =_____	11 − 8 = _____	15 − 7 = _____
8 + 12 =_____	12 + 8 =_____	13 − 8 = _____	19 − 11 = _____

USING DOMINOS FOR OUR MATH CLASS

Find the answers for the problems below then write the rest of the fact family.

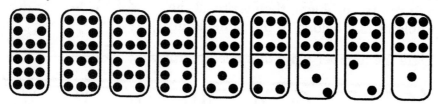

"You can also practice all of the add facts by adding both sides of the dominos as you turn them up."

"Can you make up an addition or subtraction game using dominos?"

1. _____ put all of the dominos with 8 dots on the table. Each student took a domino, and told the total number of dots. _____ 's had 8 dots and 6 dots. What was the total?

2. _____ had a domino with 8 dots and 8 more on the other side. How many dots?

3. _____ picked a domino with 5 dots and 8 dots. What was the sum of the two numbers?

4. _____'s domino had 8 dots and 7 dots. How many dots all together?

5. _____ picked a domino with 9 dots and 8 dots. How many dots?

6. The domino with 8 dots and 3 dots was left on the table. What is the answer for 8 + 3?

7. The only other domino with 8 dots that _____ could find had 2 dots on the other side. Write the math problem for it.

NAME _____ #

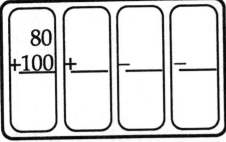

80 FACT FAMILY

Use what you know to find the answer for each printed problem, then write all the problems that belong to the same family.

Circle the add and subtract regrouping pairs.

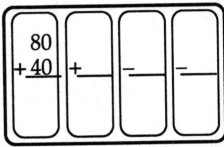

"I'm on my way to becoming a champion!"

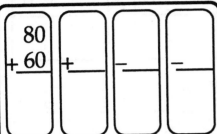

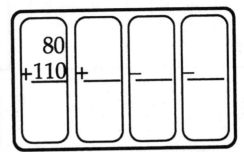

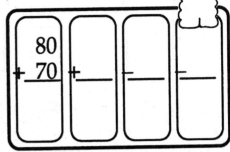

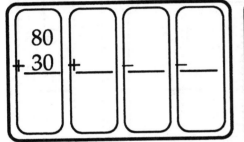

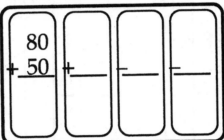

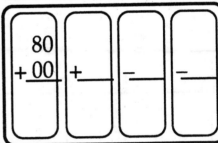

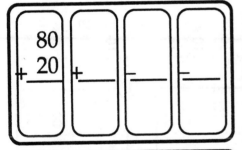

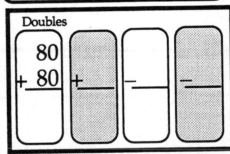

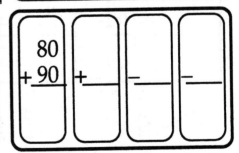

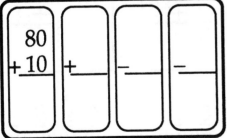

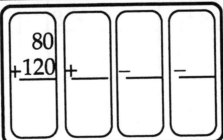

review

80 + 70 = ____	80 + 80 = ____	140 − 80 = ____	160 − 80 = ____
80 + 40 = ____	90 + 80 = ____	100 − 80 = ____	110 − 30 = ____
80 + 80 = ____	60 + 80 = ____	120 − 80 = ____	140 − 60 = ____
80 + 90 = ____	40 + 80 = ____	90 − 80 = ____	150 − 70 = ____
80 + 50 = ____	50 + 80 = ____	110 − 80 = ____	120 − 40 = ____
80 + 60 = ____	70 + 80 = ____	130 − 80 = ____	100 − 20 = ____

ADDITION   Use your Dollar, Dime and Penny Chart if you need help.

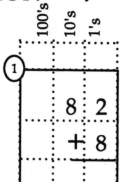

"Just a second while I think it through."

	100's	10's	1's
1		8	2
		+	8

	100's	10's	1's
2		7	3
		+	8

	100's	10's	1's
3		4	4
		+	8

	100's	10's	1's
4		3	5
		+	8

	100's	10's	1's
5		2	6
		+	8

	1000's	100's	10's	1's
6			6	7
			+	8

	1000's	100's	10's	1's
7			8	8
			+	8

	1000's	100's	10's	1's
8			4	9
			+	8

	1000's	100's	10's	1's
9			1	5
			+	8

	1000's	100's	10's	1's
10			3	3
			+	8

	1000's	100's	10's	1's
11			4	2
			+	8

	1000's	100's	10's	1's
12			5	3
			+	8

	1000's	100's	10's	1's
13			7	3
			+	8

	1000's	100's	10's	1's
14			6	8
			+	8

	1000's	100's	10's	1's
15			8	9
			+	8

	1000's	100's	10's	1's
16			8	8
		+	2	8

	1000's	100's	10's	1's
17			2	8
		+	8	6

	1000's	100's	10's	1's
18			1	8
		+	8	4

	1000's	100's	10's	1's
19			3	8
		+	7	8

	1000's	100's	10's	1's
20			4	8
		+	8	9

SUBTRACT   Use your Dollar, Dime and Penny Chart if you need help.

"First the Wrap-ups, then the worksheet. Wow! It's easy!"

1. 100's 10's 1's
$$\begin{array}{r} 4\ 0 \\ -\ \ 8 \\ \hline \end{array}$$

2. 100's 10's 1's
$$\begin{array}{r} 6\ 1 \\ -\ \ 8 \\ \hline \end{array}$$

3. 100's 10's 1's
$$\begin{array}{r} 3\ 2 \\ -\ \ 8 \\ \hline \end{array}$$

4. 100's 10's 1's
$$\begin{array}{r} 2\ 3 \\ -\ \ 8 \\ \hline \end{array}$$

5. 100's 10's 1's
$$\begin{array}{r} 8\ 4 \\ -\ \ 8 \\ \hline \end{array}$$

6. 1000's 100's 10's 1's
$$\begin{array}{r} 1\ 5 \\ -\ \ 8 \\ \hline \end{array}$$

7. 1000's 100's 10's 1's
$$\begin{array}{r} 4\ 6 \\ -\ \ 8 \\ \hline \end{array}$$

8. 1000's 100's 10's 1's
$$\begin{array}{r} 5\ 7 \\ -\ \ 8 \\ \hline \end{array}$$

9. 1000's 100's 10's 1's
$$\begin{array}{r} 2\ 7 \\ -\ \ 8 \\ \hline \end{array}$$

10. 1000's 100's 10's 1's
$$\begin{array}{r} 3\ 3 \\ -\ \ 8 \\ \hline \end{array}$$

11. 1000's 100's 10's 1's
$$\begin{array}{r} 9\ 2 \\ -\ \ 8 \\ \hline \end{array}$$

12. 1000's 100's 10's 1's
$$\begin{array}{r} 9\ 0 \\ -\ \ 8 \\ \hline \end{array}$$

13. 1000's 100's 10's 1's
$$\begin{array}{r} 5\ 4 \\ -\ \ 8 \\ \hline \end{array}$$

14. 1000's 100's 10's 1's
$$\begin{array}{r} 4\ 5 \\ -\ \ 8 \\ \hline \end{array}$$

15. 1000's 100's 10's 1's
$$\begin{array}{r} 3\ 6 \\ -\ \ 8 \\ \hline \end{array}$$

16. 1000's 100's 10's 1's
$$\begin{array}{r} 8\ 7 \\ -\ 1\ 8 \\ \hline \end{array}$$

17. 1000's 100's 10's 1's
$$\begin{array}{r} 5\ 7 \\ -\ 2\ 8 \\ \hline \end{array}$$

18. 1000's 100's 10's 1's
$$\begin{array}{r} 7\ 3 \\ -\ 3\ 8 \\ \hline \end{array}$$

19. 1000's 100's 10's 1's
$$\begin{array}{r} 6\ 1 \\ -\ 2\ 8 \\ \hline \end{array}$$

20. 1000's 100's 10's 1's
$$\begin{array}{r} 4\ 7 \\ -\ 1\ 8 \\ \hline \end{array}$$

A. PRACTICE THINKING 8's

Write the answers as fast as you can.

8+1= ___	5+8= ___	8+10= ___
8+3= ___	12+8= ___	8+11= ___
8+7= ___	1+8= ___	8+5= ___
8+5= ___	4+8= ___	8+1= ___
8+2= ___	3+8= ___	8+7= ___
8+11= ___	7+8= ___	8+3= ___
8+10= ___	9+8= ___	8+2= ___
8+8= ___	6+8= ___	8+12= ___
8+6= ___	2+8= ___	8+9= ___
8+12= ___	10+8= ___	8+8= ___
8+9= ___	8+8= ___	8+4= ___
8+4= ___	11+8= ___	8+6= ___

_____ _____ _____

If students are ready to be timed, do one column and write the time at the bottom. **Practice with the #8 Addition Learning Wrap-up for 5 minutes.** Fold the first column back, then write the second column as fast as you can. Repeat. Do the same activity with the regrouping pairs.

B.

Write the answers for just the regrouping pairs as fast as you can.

8+5= ___	4+8= ___	8+2= ___
8+3= ___	6+8= ___	8+9= ___
8+4= ___	5+8= ___	8+12= ___
8+6= ___	8+8= ___	8+3= ___
8+7= ___	12+8= ___	8+6= ___
8+2= ___	3+8= ___	8+5= ___
8+8= ___	7+8= ___	8+7= ___
8+12= ___	9+8= ___	8+4= ___
8+9= ___	2+8= ___	8+8= ___

_____ _____ _____

C.

Write the answers for just the regrouping pairs as fast as you can.

8+5= ___	9+8= ___	8+12= ___
8+3= ___	4+8= ___	8+6= ___
8+4= ___	7+8= ___	8+5= ___
8+6= ___	3+8= ___	8+2= ___
8+7= ___	5+8= ___	8+3= ___
8+2= ___	12+8= ___	8+4= ___
8+8= ___	2+8= ___	8+8= ___
8+12= ___	8+8= ___	8+9= ___
8+9= ___	6+8= ___	8+7= ___

_____ _____ _____

800 FACT FAMILY

Use what you know to find the answer for each printed problem, then write all the problems that belong to the same family.

Circle the add and subtract regrouping pairs.

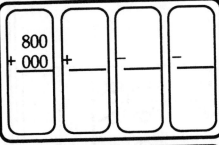

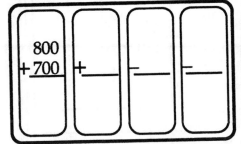

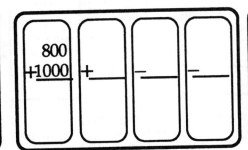

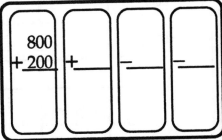

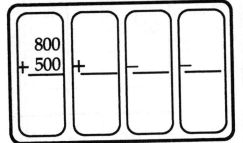

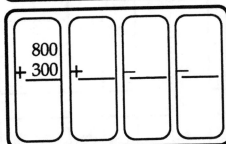

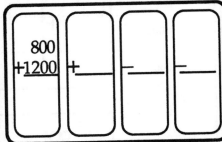

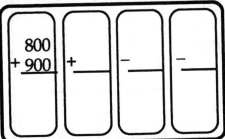

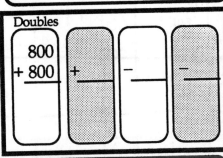

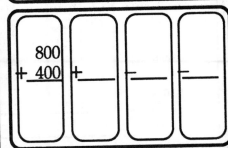

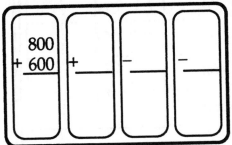

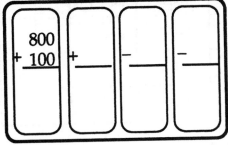

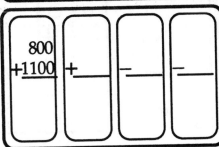

review

800 + 700 = _____	800 + 800 = _____	1400 − 800 = _____	1100 − 300 = _____
800 + 600 = _____	900 + 800 = _____	1500 − 800 = _____	1500 − 700 = _____
800 + 800 = _____	700 + 800 = _____	1200 − 800 = _____	1400 − 600 = _____
800 + 900 = _____	600 + 800 = _____	900 − 800 = _____	1600 − 800 = _____
800 + 500 = _____	400 + 800 = _____	1100 − 800 = _____	1300 − 500 = _____
800 + 400 = _____	500 + 800 = _____	1300 − 800 = _____	1700 − 900 = _____

POWER PAGE

WATCH THE SIGNS!

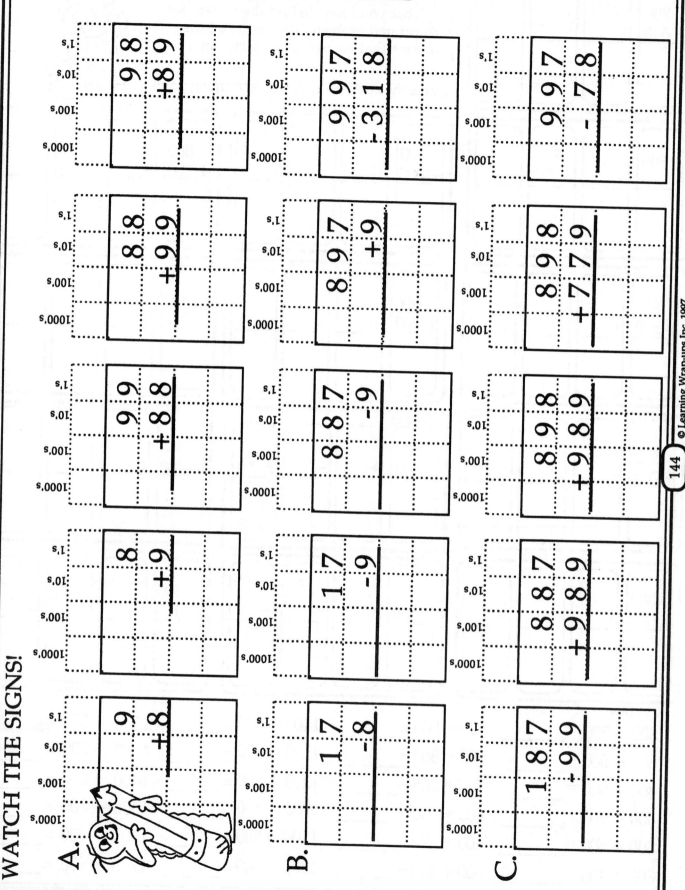

A.

```
   98        88        99         8         9
 + 89      + 92      + 88       + 9       + 8
```

B.

```
  997       897       887        17        17
 - 318      +  9      -  9       - 9       - 8
```

C.

```
  997       898       898       887       187
 -  78      +779      +989      +989      + 99
```

Two students work together. One reads the problems, the other
gives the answers from memory. Take turns reading the problems.

Watch the signs!

A.
11	20	8	0	12	16	11	8
-8	-12	+2	+8	+8	-8	-3	-6
3	8	10	8	20	8	8	2

B.
8	19	14	15	8	17	8	8
+8	-11	-8	-7	-7	-8	+11	-4
16	8	6	8	1	9	19	4

C.
15	8	7	10	13	1	8	8
-8	-0	+8	-2	-5	+8	+4	+5
7	8	15	8	8	9	12	13

D.
3	5	19	18	8	10	10	8
+8	+8	-8	-10	+7	-8	+8	-5
11	13	11	8	15	2	18	3

E.
80	80	120	160	80	80	80	80
-10	+80	-80	-80	+30	+90	+120	-30
70	160	40	80	110	170	200	50

F.
110	180	170	80	60	80	90	80
+80	-80	-90	+10	+80	-80	-10	+60
190	100	80	90	140	00	80	140

Can you remember how to say the numbers that have a number in the thousands column?

G.
900	1300	1400	800	400	900	1200	800
+800	-800	-600	-200	+800	-800	-400	+1000
1700	500	800	600	1200	100	800	1800

+ - 8 THINKER SHEET

© Learning Wrap-ups Inc. 1997

LESSON PLANS FOR TEACHING + - 9

1. Have students put all the Wrap-ups in order and in sets.   Collect them.

2. Students should be able to do all the 9 facts at this point. Check HERE'S WHAT I KNOW, p. 18.

3. TALK ABOUT how much the students have learned. Ask if anyone can think of a 9 fact that has not yet been learned. Tell them you are going to give the + - 9 QUICK QUIZ first this time.

   Explain that you know they haven't had time to practice with the #9 **Wrap-ups**, but you will allow extra time for them to think about Commutative Partners and the inverse operation of subtraction as they are doing the quiz.

4. Most of the students will do well with the quiz. If they need more 9's practice, use the + - 9 pages that follow as needed.

5. SEND HOME the complete set of Addition Learning Wrap-ups. Tell them to practice doing all 10 boards as fast as they can. Tell them you will be giving the Post Test the following day.

6. Give the Pre/Post Test for 6, 7, 8, 9, and 10, p. 24. Tell students to do the ADDITION problems first, then work on the subtraction.

7. SEND HOME the Subtraction Wrap-ups and GIVE THE SAME TEST again the next day. This time tell students to do the SUBTRACTION problems first.

8. The practice from doing the test twice will be beneficial to the students.

NEXT DAY

- Do something wonderful!

- Have a party, give out treats, take an extra recess, anything to let students know it's time for celebration. Tell them how much you appreciate how hard they have been working.

- Extol the benefits students will reap from the efforts they have put forth.

- If you solicited help from the local merchants, invite some of them to come share in the celebration.

- All parents who have been involved should join in the fun, too.

- By all means, invite the principal.

KEEPING SHARP

- Students should now be able to move through their regular textbook at an amazing pace. Whenever they need a quick review of the facts, or a particular concept, go back in this book and pull out the necessary pages.

- Have a weekly WRAP-OFF! Make large A D D and S U B T R A C T words to place on your classroom door. Have all the students who did the WRAP-OFF in goal time sign them.

- SEND HOME specific WRAP-UPS for practice if a student is experiencing a certain fact problem.

- Every time you have a few seconds' time, while students are lining up, cleaning up, etc, ask them to give answers to math fact problems.

COVER THE CIRCLES WITH PENNIES OR DISCS TO COMPLETE THESE PROBLEMS.

+ 9 PENNY PAGE

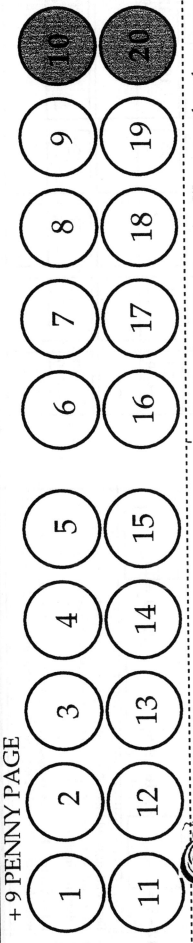

1	2	3	4	5	6	7	8	9	10
11	12	13	14	15	16	17	18	19	20

A.

"Are you looking closely at the dark printed problems? They are number pairs that total 10 or more. Think about them in your mind. Close your eyes, then say each problem and answer aloud."

Use pennies or discs to solve these problems.

1 + 9 =	5 + 9 =	9 + 9 =
2 + 9 =	6 + 9 =	10 + 9 =
3 + 9 =	7 + 9 =	11 + 9 =
4 + 9 =	8 + 9 =	12 + 9 =

Each student should have 20 discs or pennies. Make certain all the problems in section A are correct. Students do not have enough pennies or circles to do the last problem. Ask what they can do about it. Watch to see if students have picked up on commutative property, by laying the largest number of discs down first, then adding the smaller number.
Work with the **#9 Addition Learning Wrap-ups,** doing them several times. Remind students about commutative property of addition, and have them do section B.

Do the **#9 Addition Learning Wrap-up** and mark a square each time you do it correctly.

☒ ☐ ☐ ☐ ☐ ☐ ☐ ☐

B. Work these problems down the columns instead of across. Can you do them without covering the circles?

1 + 9	2 + 9	3 + 9	4 + 9	5 + 9	6 + 9
7 + 9	8 + 9	9 + 9	10 + 9	11 + 9	12 + 9
9 + 1	9 + 4	9 +10	9 + 7	9 + 8	9 + 5
9 + 12	9 + 2	9 + 3	9 + 6	9 + 9	9 +11

USE PENNIES OR DISCS ON THE CIRCLES TO COMPLETE THESE PROBLEMS

NAME _____

- 9 PENNY PAGE

Always start at 1 when covering the number circles to solve problems.
To take away or subtract, remove discs or pennies starting from the last circle you covered.

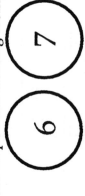

1	2	3	4	5	6	7	8	9
11	12	13	14	15	16	17	18	19

(circles 10 and 20 shaded)

A. Use pennies or discs to solve these problems if you need to.

"Just thinking of what I know about the addition facts can help me with subtraction!"

9 - 9 =		13 - 9 =		17 - 9 =	
10 - 9 =		14 - 9 =		18 - 9 =	
11 - 9 =		15 - 9 =		19 - 9 =	
12 - 9 =		16 - 9 =		20 - 9 =	

Each student should have 20 pennies. Be certain students have all the answers in section A correct. Continue to emphasize that any number subtracted from itself equals 0.

Do #9 Subtract Learning Wrap-up, saying problems and answers aloud several times. Then fold the paper and do section B for additional practice.

Do the **#9 Subtraction Learning Wrap-up** and mark a square each time you do it correctly.
☒ ☐ ☐ ☐ ☐ ☐ ☐ ☐ ☐ ☐ ☐

B. Can you do these problems without using pennies or discs? Work problems down the columns, instead of across.

9 − 9	10 − 9	11 − 9	12 − 9	13 − 9	14 − 9
15 − 9	16 − 9	17 − 9	18 − 9	19 − 9	20 − 9
14 − 9	9 − 9	13 − 9	15 − 9	19 − 9	12 − 9
16 − 9	10 − 9	18 − 9	20 − 9	11 − 9	17 − 9

148

COMMUTATIVE PARTNERS   SUBTRACTION BUDDIES

$1+9=$ ___	$9+1=$ ___	$10-9=$ ___	$10-1=$ ___
$2+9=$ ___	$9+2=$ ___	$11-9=$ ___	$11-2=$ ___
$3+9=$ ___	$9+3=$ ___	$12-9=$ ___	$12-3=$ ___
$4+9=$ ___	$9+4=$ ___	$13-9=$ ___	$13-4=$ ___
$5+9=$ ___	$9+5=$ ___	$14-9=$ ___	$14-5=$ ___
$6+9=$ ___	$9+6=$ ___	$15-9=$ ___	$15-6=$ ___
$7+9=$ ___	$9+7=$ ___	$16-9=$ ___	$16-7=$ ___
$8+9=$ ___	$9+8=$ ___	$17-9=$ ___	$17-8=$ ___
$9+9=$ ___	$9+9=$ ___	$18-9=$ ___	$18-9=$ ___
$10+9=$ ___	$9+10=$ ___	$19-9=$ ___	$19-10=$ ___
$11+9=$ ___	$9+11=$ ___	$20-9=$ ___	$20-11=$ ___
$12+9=$ ___	$9+12=$ ___	$21-9=$ ___	$21-12=$ ___

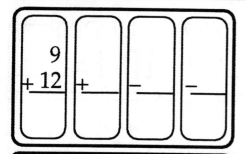

9 FACT FAMILY

Use what you know to find the answer for each printed problem, then write all the problems that belong to the same family.

"It's like magic when you know the facts."

Circle the addition and subtraction regrouping pairs.

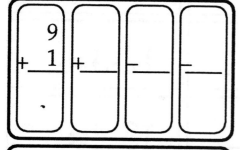

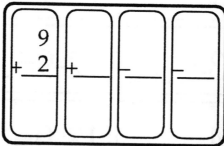

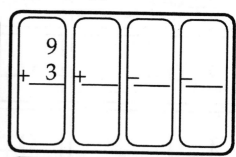

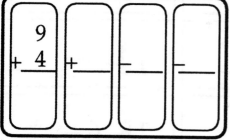

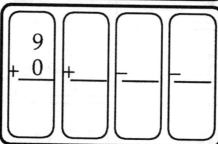

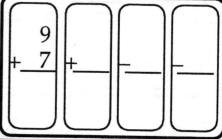

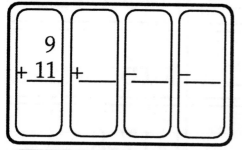

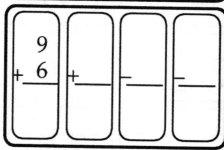

Doubles

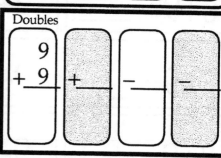

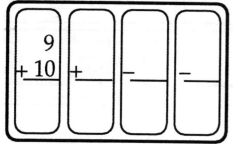

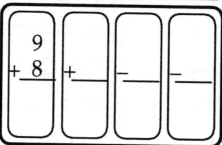

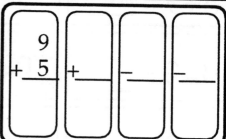

review

9 + 7 = ____	8 + 9 = ____	14 − 9 = ____	21 − 12 = ____
9 + 10 = ____	9 + 9 = ____	10 − 9 = ____	18 − 9 = ____
9 + 8 = ____	7 + 9 = ____	12 − 9 = ____	17 − 8 = ____
9 + 9 = ____	10 + 9 = ____	9 − 9 = ____	19 − 10 = ____
9 + 11 = ____	11 + 9 = ____	11 − 9 = ____	16 − 7 = ____
9 + 12 = ____	12 + 9 = ____	13 − 9 = ____	20 − 11 = ____

USING MANIPULATIVES

Our teacher has a box full of manipulatives. Each of us picked out the ones we wanted to use, then made up a problem. We also wrote the Commutative Partner and the Subtraction Buddies to go with it.

1. _____had 9 green buttons and 5 yellow ones. How many buttons did she have?

   _____   _____

   _____   _____

2. _____ had 6 little plastic zoo animals and 9 farm animals. How many animals all together?

   _____   _____

   _____   _____

3. _____used the cubes for his problem. He had 9 cubes in one stack and 8 cubes in the other. Write his problem and answer.

   _____   _____

   _____   _____

4. _____ found short strings of beads. One string had 7 beads. The other one had 9 beads. Write the problems to go with the strings of beads.

   _____   _____

   _____   _____

5. _____ chose to take the wooden pegs. There were 9 red pegs and 4 orange pegs. Write the problems.

   _____   _____

   _____   _____

6. There were lots of plastic shapes. _____chose 12 triangles and 9 squares. How many plastic shapes were there? Write all the problems and answers to go with these facts.

   _____   _____

   _____   _____

7. _____picked the plastic teddy bears. There were 10 big ones and 9 little ones. How many total?

   _____   _____

   _____   _____

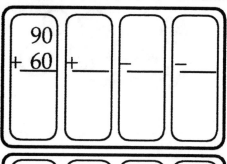

90 FACT FAMILY

"Almost done! Isn't it nice?"

Use what you know to find the answer for each printed problem, then write all the problems that belong to the same family.

Circle the number pairs that need to be regrouped.

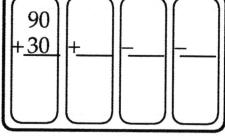

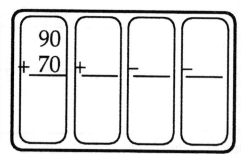

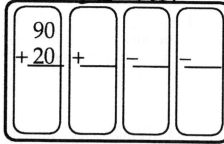

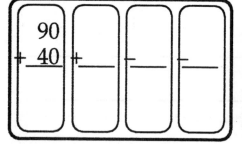

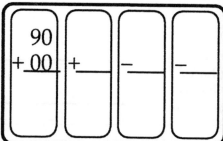

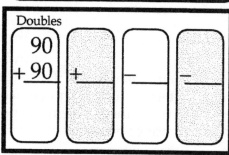

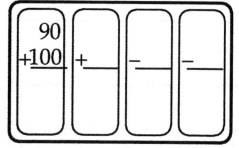

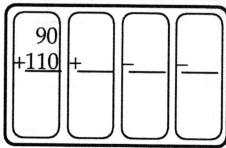

Doubles

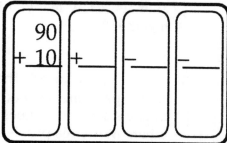

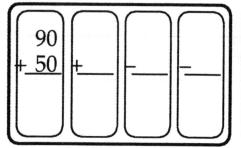

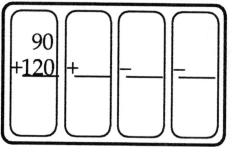

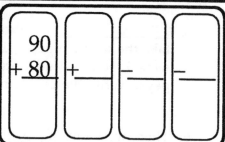

review

90 + 70 = _____	80 + 90 = _____	140 − 90 = _____	160 − 70 = _____
90 + 40 = _____	90 + 90 = _____	100 − 90 = _____	110 − 20 = _____
90 + 80 = _____	60 + 90 = _____	120 − 90 = _____	140 − 50 = _____
90 + 90 = _____	40 + 90 = _____	90 − 90 = _____	150 − 60 = _____
90 + 50 = _____	50 + 90 = _____	110 − 90 = _____	120 − 30 = _____
90 + 60 = _____	70 + 90 = _____	130 − 90 = _____	100 − 10 = _____

ADD Use your Dollars, Dimes and Pennies Chart if you need help.

"I've noticed something unusual about adding 9's. Have you?"

"The 10's column goes up one number and the 1's column goes down one number!"

1. 21 + 9

2. 42 + 9

3. 63 + 9

4. 54 + 9

5. 45 + 9

6. 86 + 9

7. 77 + 9

8. 38 + 9

9. 29 + 9

10. 12 + 9

11. 23 + 9

12. 34 + 9

13. 46 + 9

14. 65 + 9

15. 59 + 9

16. 149 + 38

17. 209 + 83

18. 469 + 19

19. 79 + 19

20. 69 + 19

SUBTRACT Use your Dollars, Dimes and Pennies Chart if you need help.

"Have you noticed that when you subtract 9 from a 2 digit number, the 10's column goes down one number and the 1's column goes up one number?

Just the opposite of adding! WOW!"

1) 11 − 9

2) 42 − 9

3) 63 − 9

4) 24 − 9

5) 35 − 9

6) 86 − 9

7) 97 − 9

8) 78 − 9

9) 20 − 9

10) 31 − 9

11) 46 − 9

12) 52 − 9

13) 73 − 9

14) 34 − 9

15) 28 − 9

16) 83 − 19

17) 43 − 29

18) 65 − 49

19) 91 − 69

20) 80 − 39

A. Which number pair does NOT need to be regrouped?

9+5=	4+9=	12+9=	1+9=	9+5=
9+3=	6+9=	9+1=	5+9=	9+3=
9+4=	5+9=	2+9=	7+9=	9+7=
9+6=	8+9=	9+5=	9+4=	9+9=
9+7=	12+9=	6+9=	9+6=	9+1=
9+2=	3+9=	4+9=	9+12=	9+10=
9+8=	7+9=	8+9=	3+9=	9+8=
9+12=	9+9=	9+11=	9+9=	9+12=
9+9=	2+9=	9+3=	9+2=	9+4=
9+11=	1+9=	10+9=	9+10=	9+11=
9+1=	10+9=	9+7=	11+9=	9+6=
9+10=	11+9=	9+9=	9+8=	9+2=

B.

2+9=	12+9=	11+9=	9+8=	9+11=
9+11=	7+9=	1+9=	9+1=	9+9=
12+9=	4+9=	9+10=	9+10=	10+9=
4+9=	3+9=	9+9=	9+3=	9+7=
10+9=	11+9=	7+9=	9+12=	8+9=
9+5=	6+9=	9+2=	9+5=	12+9=
6+9=	1+9=	9+4=	9+11=	9+5=
9+9=	10+9=	3+9=	9+7=	9+1=
8+9=	9+9=	5+9=	9+4=	9+3=
9+7=	2+9=	9+6=	9+2=	6+9=
9+1=	5+9=	9+12=	9+6=	4+9=
9+3=	8+9=	9+8=	9+9=	2+9=

POWER PAGE 9+6

WATCH THE SIGNS!

Column headers for each grid: 1's · 10's · 100's · 1000's

A.

$$96 + 69$$

$$66 + 99$$

$$99 + 66$$

$$96 + 9$$

$$69 + 6$$

B.

$$996 - 629$$

$$995 - 909$$

$$996 - 619$$

$$95 - 9$$

$$65 - 9$$

C.

$$195 - 69$$

$$969 + 696$$

$$696 + 969$$

$$556 + 999$$

$$166 + 99$$

Two students work together. One reads the problems, the other gives the answers from memory. Take turns reading the problems.

Watch the signs!

0 +9 9	19 -10 9	4 +9 13	13 -4 9	6 +9 15	14 -9 5	16 -7 9	9 +11 20
9 -3 6	9 +1 10	3 +9 12	9 +3 12	18 -9 9	9 +9 18	10 -1 9	9 +12 21
19 -9 10	1 +9 10	9 -4 5	9 -2 7	14 -5 9	9 -9 0	8 +9 17	17 -9 8
9 -1 8	9 +8 17	15 -6 9	13 -9 4	12 +9 21	9 -8 1	9 +6 15	11 -2 9
20 -11 9	15 -9 6	50 +90 140	90 +50 140	90 -60 30	9 -0 9	11 -9 2	10 +9 19
90 -70 20	110 +90 200	120 -90 30	120 -30 90	90 +100 190	180 -90 90	90 +90 180	160 -90 70
900 -500 400	210 -100 110	900 +700 1600	1000 -900 100	700 +900 1600	900 -200 700	900 +400 1300	1700 -800 900

+ - 9 THINKER SHEET

WHAT NUMBER IS MISSING?

- Fill in the missing number in each of the boxes.
- Teacher calls for a family at a certain address (example: 6a, 5c, 2h, etc.) Students find the number box, determine whether to add or subtract and call out or write down the missing number.
- All of the answers are part of the Addition/Subtraction Fact Family.
- For this page, "0" cannot be an answer.
- Hint: None of the answers can be greater than 19.
- If a number on top is less than a number in the middle, you must add.

1.

a	b	c	d	e	f	g	h	i	j	k	l	m
2	4	16	5	5	2	4	10		4	3	13	16
	8			7		4		9	9	3	8	
4		10	11		6		8	13	9			8

2.

a	b	c	d	e	f	g	h	i	j	k	l	m
13	11		18	17	16	9		14	13		10	2
		9		9	8		9		8	6		
5	4	3	9			12	6	8		7	3	4

3.

a	b	c	d	e	f	g	h	i	j	k	l	m
12		15	9	16		7		16	8		10	7
	7	5			9		6	9	7			
6	7	6		8	8	17	2		5	8	5	16

4.

a	b	c	d	e	f	g	h	i	j	k	l	m
	12	2	8		13	9	9	3	1	17	14	7
6		5		4		10		11	2	9		
5	5		4	2	9		3				8	16

5.

a	b	c	d	e	f	g	h	i	j	k	l	m
5	6		8	9	5	6			5			18
5		9	9	9		7	9	8		6	7	
	13	16			13		15	14	13	13	10	9

6.

a	b	c	d	e	f	g	h	i	j	k	l	m
6	5	8	8	3	14	7	2		3		6	14
6		8		4	6	9		7	5	8	8	
	14		17				10	14		15		6

We hereby recognize

_____
student

as a MATH CHAMPION who

set a goal to

LEARN THE
ADDITION AND SUBTRACTION FACTS

and has

Successfully Met The Goal!

_____
teacher

_____
principal

_____
school

_____
grade

_____
date

Learning Wrap-up ® Seal of Success

Answers for Pre/post test 1-5 facts p. 23

subtract

1	6	1	12	2
3	11	4	6	12
9	5	12	11	7
6	2	9	3	1
7	12	8	9	10
4	1	11	4	5
10	10	3	2	9
3	3	6	10	11
11	8	7	1	4
12	4	10	7	8
8	9	5	5	6
5	7	2	8	3

add

2	4	6	8	17
4	7	10	10	15
10	14	14	12	12
7	3	8	15	10
11	7	11	5	9
3	8	7	13	14
12	12	9	7	13
5	10	5	16	11
9	13	15	6	8
13	5	4	14	7
8	9	12	9	16
6	6	13	11	6

Answers for Pre/post test 6-10 facts p. 24

subtract

12	10	4	11	7
7	1	12	1	12
3	12	3	12	1
9	8	5	10	4
4	2	7	2	10
11	3	6	9	5
1	4	1	4	11
10	7	9	7	6
5	11	2	8	3
6	6	8	5	8
8	9	11	3	2
2	5	10	6	9

add

7	14	9	15	16
11	8	15	10	11
8	10	20	21	22
18	13	12	14	12
14	16	10	18	18
17	9	14	11	19
15	19	11	20	15
12	18	18	13	13
10	12	19	19	14
16	15	16	16	21
9	11	17	12	17
13	17	13	17	20

Answers for Quick Quizzes

1's		2's (page 25)		3's		4's		5's (page 26)		6's		7's		8's (page 27)		9's	
2	5	5	7	11	4	5	2	8	4	14	1	8	10	11	1	17	11
9	7	9	8	4	12	12	4	12	5	7	9	15	1	15	2	10	6
6	10	3	1	6	3	9	7	6	10	9	10	12	4	9	12	12	7
3	1	14	9	8	9	6	10	17	6	11	6	9	7	20	3	14	3
11	9	7	3	15	1	14	6	10	11	18	11	17	3	13	8	21	8
8	2	12	2	13	8	11	11	15	12	16	5	14	8	18	7	19	2
10	4	6	12	5	7	13	1	9	9	8	4	16	11	12	6	11	1
4	6	10	10	9	5	7	3	13	7	12	2	10	12	16	4	15	10
12	12	13	11	7	11	15	9	16	8	10	8	18	6	19	5	13	5
7	8	4	5	12	10	10	5	7	2	15	7	13	2	10	11	18	4
13	11	8	4	14	6	16	8	11	1	17	3	19	5	14	9	20	12
5	3	11	6	10	2	8	12	14	3	13	12	11	9	17	10	16	9

Answers for Regrouping Pages

Prob#	1	2	3	4	5	6	7	8	9	10	11	12	13	14	15	16	17	18	19	20
p. 75	30	62	51	31	52	17	29	38	29	37	19	42	61	27	48	39	32	81	69	80
p. 86	20	41	52	63	20	31	61	52	90	103	16	27	38	49	59	26	57	48	39	76
p. 97	30	41	52	33	64	72	31	24	93	102	40	53	42	53	31	339	427	627	518	236
p. 98	25	36	47	28	59	15	27	16	39	18	49	65	25	76	89	386	173	493	191	552
p. 114	30	41	82	33	54	50	21	35	35	34	44	25	31	43	54	405	339	590	492	209
p. 115	14	25	36	47	58	69	74	15	25	36	75	47	68	39	26	19	18	26	55	226
p. 127	40	31	62	33	24	55	76	30	41	52	133	137	95	96	101	102	93	84	85	86
p. 128	3	24	35	56	77	18	49	26	19	28	35	35	37	24	23	17	19	68	37	16
p. 140	90	81	52	43	34	75	96	57	23	41	50	61	81	76	97	116	114	102	116	137
p. 141	32	53	24	15	76	7	38	49	19	25	84	82	46	37	28	69	29	35	33	29
p. 153	30	51	72	63	54	95	86	47	38	21	32	43	55	74	68	187	292	488	98	88
p. 154	2	33	54	15	26	77	88	69	11	22	37	43	64	25	19	64	14	16	22	41

Who's Missing? Answers p. 158

	a	b	c	d	e	f	g	h	i	j	k	l	m
1.	2	12	6	6	12	4	8	2	4	5	6	5	8
2.	8	7	12	9	8	8	3	15	6	5	13	7	2
3.	6	14	9	4	8	17	10	8	7	3	15	5	9
4.	11	7	7	4	6	4	19	6	14	3	8	6	9
5.	10	7	7	17	18	8	13	6	6	8	7	3	9
6.	12	9	16	9	7	8	16	8	7	8	7	14	8

© Learning Wrap-ups Inc. 1997